PRINCIPALS Matter

PRINCIPALS
Matter

A Guide to School, Family, and Community Partnerships

Mavis G. Sanders • Steven B. Sheldon

CORWIN
A SAGE Company

For information:

Corwin
A SAGE Company
2455 Teller Road
Thousand Oaks, California 91320
(800) 233-9936
Fax: (800) 417-2466
www.corwinpress.com

SAGE India Pvt. Ltd.
B 1/I 1 Mohan Cooperative
    Industrial Area
Mathura Road, New Delhi 110 044
India

SAGE Ltd.
1 Oliver's Yard
55 City Road
London EC1Y 1SP
United Kingdom

SAGE Asia-Pacific Pte. Ltd.
33 Pekin Street #02-01
Far East Square
Singapore 048763

Printed in the United States of America

Library of Congress Cataloging-in-Publication Data

Sanders, Mavis G.
Principals matter: a guide to school, family, and community partnerships/Mavis G. Sanders and Steven B. Sheldon.
      p. cm.
Includes bibliographical references and index.
ISBN 978-1-4129-6041-0 (cloth)
ISBN 978-1-4129-6042-7 (pbk.)

   1. School principals—Professional relationships—United States. 2. Home and school—United States. 3. Community and school—United States. I. Sheldon, Steven B. II. Title.

LB2831.92.S26 2009
371.2'012—dc22   2008054113

This book is printed on acid-free paper.

09   10   11   12   13   10   9   8   7   6   5   4   3   2   1

Acquisitions Editor:	Arnis Burvikovs
Associate Editor:	Desirée A. Bartlett
Production and Copy Editor:	Jane Haenel
Typesetter:	C&M Digitals (P) Ltd.
Proofreader:	Theresa Kay
Indexer:	Wendy Allex
Cover and Graphic Designer:	Karine Hovsepian

Contents

Acknowledgments

We would like to extend special thanks to the staff of the National Network of Partnership Schools (NNPS). We would especially like to thank the director, Dr. Joyce L. Epstein, for her seminal work in the field of school, family, and community partnerships, as well as her guidance, leadership, and friendship. We would also like to thank NNPS facilitators Marsha Greenfeld, Darcy Hutchins, and Brenda Thomas; NNPS Coordinator Jenn Ganss; NNPS Research Consultant Dr. Frances Van Voorhis; and the school, district, state, and organization members of NNPS. They have individually and collectively made profound contributions to research and practice in the field of school, family, and community partnerships. We are especially thankful to those school and district leaders whose successes, challenges, and insights are shared in this book. We are also indebted to Corwin, especially to Arnis Burvikovs, Desirée Bartlett, and Jane Haenel, the team that oversaw the small and large steps essential to making this book a reality.

I would also like to thank the students in my courses on leadership for school, family, and community partnerships, especially Carydad Morales for her insights into working with LEP families. Our interaction continues to broaden and deepen my understanding of and commitment to partnerships as best practice in education. In addition, I would like to thank my parents, Grover and Vera Sanders, my sisters, Desiree, Vetta, Pamela, and Camilla, my wonderful nieces and nephews, and my beautiful and inspiring children, Shori and B.J., for their constant love and support.

—MGS

I would like to thank Frances, with whom I have had many discussions about the important work of principals and their vital role in the successful development and implementation of school, family, and community partnership programs. In addition, I am grateful to my parents, Samuel and Beverly Sheldon, whose involvement in my own life has been an inspiration to me and whose support has been unconditional, and to my brother David, who has been a role model, a skeptic, and an additional source of support. Finally, I would like to thank my wonderful children, Evan and Mara, who have anchored my interest and work on family involvement in the real, everyday experiences of my life. All of these individuals have provided me with endless love, motivation, and enthusiasm for this work.

—SBS

PUBLISHER'S ACKNOWLEDGMENTS

Corwin gratefully acknowledges the contributions of the following individuals:

Julie C. Burger, Principal
Frederick Leighton Elementary
  School
Oswego, NY

Marian Hermie, Clinical Associate
  Professor
Arizona State University
Tempe, AZ

Catherine Bushbacher, Principal
Reinberg Elementary School
Chicago, IL

William Ruff, Assistant Professor
Montana State University
Bozeman, MT

Carol S. Cash, Professor
Virginia Tech
Blacksburg, VA

Stephen Shepperd, Principal
Sunnyside Elementary School
Kellogg, ID

Nora Friedman, Principal
South Grove Elementary School
Syosset, NY

Emily Shoemaker, Professor
University of La Verne
La Verne, CA

Belinda Gimbert, Assistant
  Professor
The Ohio State University
Columbus, OH

Steve Zsiray, Principal/CEO
InTech Collegiate High School
North Logan, UT

About the Authors

Mavis G. Sanders, PhD in education from Stanford University, holds a joint appointment as research scientist at the Center for the Social Organization of Schools (CSOS) and as associate professor in the School of Education at Johns Hopkins University. Dr. Sanders coordinates and teaches courses for a master's level certificate program in leadership for school, family, and community collaboration. She also has published and presented numerous papers on the processes and outcomes of school, family, and community connections, including articles appearing in *Teachers College Record, Urban Education*, the *Journal of Negro Education, Educational Leadership*, and the *Elementary School Journal*. She edited *Schooling Students Placed at Risk: Research, Policy, and Practice in the Education of Poor and Minority Adolescents*, which includes several chapters highlighting the importance of family and community involvement for the school success of poor students and students of color. She also is coauthor of *School, Family, and Community Partnerships: Your Handbook for Action*, which provides tools and information to assist schools, districts, and state departments of education to plan and implement programs of partnership. In 2005, she authored *Building School-Community Partnerships: Collaboration for Student Success*, also published by Corwin.

Steven B. Sheldon, PhD in educational psychology from Michigan State University, is a research scientist with the Center on School, Family, and Community Partnerships and Director of Research with the National Network of Partnership Schools at Johns Hopkins University. He has authored several research articles and book chapters about the development of family and community involvement programs in schools, the impact of partnership programs and activities on family involvement and student outcomes, and the influence of parents' social relationships and social networks on their involvement in their children's schooling. He also is coauthor of *School, Family, and Community Partnerships: Your Handbook for Action*, which provides tools and information to assist schools, districts, and state departments of education to plan and implement programs of partnership. Dr. Sheldon is interested in understanding the range of influences on parents' and family members' decisions to become involved in their children's education, including the role of social capital and the nature of school-home relationships and the impact of these decisions on students' academic and social-emotional outcomes.

Introduction

Standards for School, Family, and Community Partnerships

Today, standards for professional educational practice are propelling school, family, and community partnerships into the educational mainstream. These standards are being set forth by a variety of organizations that work with and for teachers, teacher educators, and, importantly, principals and those responsible for their preparation. These organizations (see Box 1) understand the complexity of teaching and learning and the importance of schools, families, and communities working collaboratively to ensure that all students have access to excellent instruction in nurturing responsive educational environments.

As indicated in Box 1, some of the organizations (e.g., INTASC and NBPTS) focus on classroom teachers, recognizing the important role teachers play in students' learning and in the success of home-school partnerships. Caspe (2001) observed:

> Over the next 10 years, an estimated 2.2 million new educators are expected to enter the teaching force. In the current climate of high standards and accountability these teachers bear the responsibility for the success of all students. Research clearly shows that teacher qualifications are related to student achievement. . . . Standards for the teaching profession have integrated family and community relations as areas where teachers need to demonstrate competency. Families and local communities are crucial partners to improve student achievement and teachers are expected in new professional and state standards to engage them to a much greater extent. (p. 3)

Box 1   Educational Organizations and Standards for Parent and Community Involvement

Early Childhood Learning
Communities Standards (http://web.naesp.org)

Standard 2: Engage Families and Communities: Effective principals work with families and community organizations to support children at home, in the community, and in pre-K and kindergarten programs.

Interstate New Teacher Assessment and
Support Consortium (INTASC) (http://www.ccsso.org)

Principle #10: The teacher fosters relationships with school colleagues, parents, and agencies in the larger community to support students' learning and well-being.

Interstate School Leaders Licensure
Consortium (ISLLC) (http://www.ccsso.org)

Standard 4: A school administrator is an educational leader who promotes the success of all students by collaborating with faculty and community members, responding to diverse community interests and needs, and mobilizing community resources.

National Board for Professional
Teaching Standards (NBPTS) (http://www.nbpts.org)

Proposition 5: Teachers are members of learning communities; they know how to work collaboratively with parents to engage them productively in the work of the school.

National Council for Accreditation of
Teacher Education (NCATE) (http://www.ncate.org)

Standard 1: Candidate Knowledge, Skills, and Professional Dispositions (1g. Professional Dispositions for all Candidates)

Target: Candidates work with students, families, colleagues, and communities in ways that reflect the professional dispositions expected of professional educators as delineated in professional, state, and institutional standards.

National Staff Development Council (NSDC) (http://www.nsdc.org)

Content Standards: Staff development that improves the learning of all students and provides educators with knowledge and skills to involve families and other stakeholders appropriately.

Other organizations setting professional standards for family and community involvement focus on school administrators, recognizing that principals significantly impact teachers' family and community involvement practices as well as the quality of schoolwide family and community outreach (Decker, Decker, & Brown, 2007; Epstein, 2001; Henderson, Mapp, Johnson, & Davies, 2007; Sanders & Harvey, 2002). For example, the Interstate School Leaders Licensure Consortium's (ISLLC) standards for school administrators were adopted by the Council of Chief State School Officers (CCSSO) in 1996. These six standards are aligned with the National Council for Accreditation of Teacher Education's (NCATE) curriculum guidelines for school administrators and reflect the skills, knowledge, and dispositions needed for leaders of twenty-first-century schools (CCSSO, 2008).

While the ISLLC standards generally guide school leaders to engage multiple stakeholders in the creation of safe, nurturing, and academically challenging and responsive school environments, Standard 4 specifically focuses on leadership for home, school, and community partnerships.

According to ISLLC Standard 4:

> A school administrator is an educational leader who promotes the success of all students by collaborating with faculty and community members, responding to diverse community interests and needs, and mobilizing community resources.

This book has been designed to assist administrators in meeting professional standards for leadership in school, family, and community partnerships. It draws on theories, research, and best practice to provide readers with a deep understanding of how to create school climates that support partnerships, how to ensure that partnerships respect and respond to diversity, and how to evaluate partnership programs to maximize benefits for students, families, communities, and the school. While some of the research discussed in the book is drawn from our individual and collaborative studies at the Center on School, Family, and Community Partnerships and with the National Network of Partnership Schools (NNPS),[1] both at Johns Hopkins University, we have sought to present a broad array of literature from the field.

The book is organized into three parts. The first section, Laying the Foundation, includes two chapters. The first chapter discusses research on student outcomes associated with family and community involvement and the significant influence of administrators on a variety of school outcomes, including the quality of home-school partnerships. Chapter 2

---

[1] NNPS was established in 1996 to provide schools, districts, and states with research-based guidelines and tools to develop goal-focused programs of school, family, and community partnerships.

builds on this discussion to describe how administrators can create school cultures that support partnerships. More specifically, this chapter discusses the role of schools as community institutions, defines partnerships as a school improvement effort, describes obstacles to effective partnerships, and presents steps that principals can take to create schools that support and sustain partnerships.

Part II, Responding to Diversity, includes four chapters that focus on populations that may be overlooked in partnership programs but are found in most schools. Chapter 3 focuses of the role of fathers and father-figures in children's learning and school success. Much of the current research and practice on partnerships focuses on mothers who have traditionally been most involved in children and adolescents' schooling. However, research shows the positive effects of fathers' involvement on student outcomes. This chapter discusses how schools can welcome and include fathers in their partnership efforts.

Chapter 4 focuses on the families of children with disabilities. Current legislation requires schools to involve families of children with disabilities in educational decision making. Such legislation, however, focuses more on procedure than partnerships, and the families of children with disabilities can be rendered invisible in many schools' partnership plans and activities. With focused attention, schools can ensure that these families' unique needs and concerns are not overlooked in partnership efforts and that they reap the many benefits of home-school-community collaboration.

Chapter 5 focuses on linguistically diverse families. Over the last decade, linguistic diversity and the number of Limited English Proficient (LEP) students have grown in the United States. The U.S. census defines LEP populations as individuals who speak a language other than English at home and speak English less than "very well" (Capps et al., 2005). According to census data, the LEP share of students in grades preK–5 rose from 4.7 to 7.4 percent from 1980 to 2000, while the LEP share of children in grades 6–12 rose from 3.1 to 5.5 percent. In 2000 a total of 1.7 million LEP children were in grades preK–5 and 1.6 million were in grades 6–12 (Capps et al., 2005). This chapter discusses the impact of growing linguistic diversity on home-school interaction and No Child Left Behind (NCLB) requirements for school outreach to LEP families. It also describes strategies schools can use to build stronger ties with linguistically diverse families and communities, and the importance of culturally intelligent leadership for their successful implementation.

Finally, Chapter 6 focuses on families living in poverty. Twenty percent of children under the age of six live in poor families; 16 percent of children age six or older live in poor families (NCCP, n.d.). The National Center for Children in Poverty reports that about 39 percent of the nation's children live in families with low incomes, that is, incomes below twice the official poverty level (for 2008, about $42,000 for a family of four). Poverty is a significant predictor of low academic achievement, school failure, and high school drop out. Chapter 6 focuses on how schools can create partnerships to support the educational success of low-income children and adolescents. The chapter describes school activities to support families living in and near poverty, as well as activities that can be implemented with the support of community organizations and resources.

Part III, Maximizing Outcomes, includes a chapter on evaluating programs of school, family, and community partnerships. Partnership programs that make a difference for students' school outcomes must be linked to school goals for students, evaluated, and refined over time. Chapter 7 provides practical recommendations on how schools can ensure that their partnership efforts produce desired results for schools, communities, families, and most important, students. The conclusion describes how, through the strategies presented in this book, administrators can meet and exceed professional standards for leadership in school, family, and community partnerships. This chapter also includes a list of organizations that can support schools in their efforts to maximize the results of partnerships.

Educational standards and policies have established school, family, and community partnerships as a critical component of educational excellence. These standards and policies have also raised the bar for action and leadership to ensure that partnerships realize their full potential. In this book, we have strived to provide school leaders with information, examples, tools, and resources that can be used so that partnership programs are goal-focused, equitable, sustainable, and effective. In other words, we have attempted to provide educational leaders with a guidebook to develop the kinds of partnership programs that we wish for our children's schools and for the schools of all children.

PART I

*Laying the
Foundation*

1

Policy, Theory,
and Research on
School, Family, and
Community Partnerships

In this chapter, we discuss policy, theory, and research on school, family, and community partnerships. This chapter should provide you with a sense of the extensive literature on family and community involvement, and the different outcomes these behaviors affect.

Passage of the No Child Left Behind (NCLB) Act in 2002 aimed, among other things, to raise overall student achievement and reduce ethnicity- and income-based disparities in school achievement. To accomplish these goals, NCLB mandates a wide range of mechanisms including regular standardized testing of students, the presence of high-quality teachers in classrooms, and increased parental involvement in students' education. The law distinguishes between two forms of parent involvement, one revolving around school choice and the other focusing on improving home-school relationships.

Much of the educational research and discourse about NCLB has focused on the pros and cons of testing standards and requirements (Linn & Haug, 2002), teacher qualifications (Smith, Desimone, & Ueno, 2006), and school choice (Belfield & Levin, 2002; Goldhaber & Eide, 2002; Neild, 2005). The topic of school, family, and community partnerships, however, has generated relatively little discussion, despite surveys indicating that new teachers rate interactions with parents as one of the most stressful aspects of their jobs (MetLife, 2005). The part of NCLB mandating that schools and school districts receiving Title I funds set up processes and structures to include more families in their children's education remains overshadowed in most discussions about the efficacy of this legislation.

Title I, Sec. 1118 of NCLB requires that schools receiving funds for serving students from low-income families implement activities to help foster greater family and community involvement. For example, schools are required to create policies stating that family and community involvement are valued goals at the school, to include families on school decision- and policy-making committees, to provide information that helps parents understand academic content and achievement standards, to train educators in how to reach out to parents and implement programs connecting home and school, and to communicate in languages and at reading levels accessible to all families. In addition, NCLB encourages schools to develop partnerships with community-based organizations and businesses to help all students learn and achieve in school.

The inclusion of family involvement in federal education policy is not new and is based on previous legislative efforts to incorporate decades of theory and empirical research. Since the mid-1960s, federal education legislation has included some language about the need for schools to involve families in their children's education. As our theoretical and empirical understanding about the effects of family involvement has evolved, so has family involvement legislation.

Many theorists have long recognized the important role strong school-home connections play in child development and education. Bronfenbrenner (1979), for example, argued that children's behavior and development are influenced by their interactions within their homes, schools, and communities, and also by the "social interconnections between settings, including joint participation, communication, and the existence of information in each setting about the other" (p. 6). Also, Epstein's (2001) Theory of Overlapping Spheres of Influence argues that a child's home and school environments each have a unique influence on her or his development. However, it is the degree to which adults in these settings maintain positive relationships with one another that is critical to her or his academic success.

Beyond theory, scientific evidence supports the inclusion of school, family, and community partnerships in efforts to reform education.

Research on effective schools, those where students are learning and achieving at high levels despite what might be expected given family and neighborhood trends of low socioeconomic status (i.e., high performing–high poverty), has consistently shown that these schools have positive school-home relationships (Chrispeels, 1996; Hoffman, 1991; Purkey & Smith, 1983; Taylor, Pearson, Clark, & Walpole, 1999; Teddlie & Reynolds, 2000). More important, these high-performing schools put forth strong efforts to reach out and work with their students' families.

Other studies looking at the ability of school reform to positively affect students have also demonstrated the need for school leaders to develop strong relationships with families and community members. Rosenholz (1989) found that schools "moving" in a positive direction were actively working to bridge students' homes and schools. In contrast, schools that showed no improvement were characterized by a feeling among the staff that there was nothing they could do to engage students' families. Similar findings have been reported in studies investigating school reform in Chicago (Bryk & Schneider, 2002; Bryk, Sebring, Kerbow, Rollow, & Easton, 1998). Effective and improving schools understand the important role parents play in teachers' ability to foster student learning and academic growth.

The benefits of school-home relationships are based on the development of trust between parents and educators. Bryk and Schneider (2002) argued that schools are successful when there are strong and positive relationships among teachers, students, parents, and the community. They also argued that these relationships are especially important in urban settings, where trust across the school community is a critical resource allowing teachers, students, and parents to succeed. In areas where schools have not traditionally promoted student achievement and success, principals and other leaders need to build programs that bridge home and school, enabling families to have faith in their children's school and to support academic excellence.

Even before children enter school, their interactions with their parents and other significant adults shape language and cognitive development. Families provide "environments for literacy" where children are engaged in literacy activities such as being encouraged to talk and sing, reading books with an adult, and writing letters (Edwards, Pleasants, & Franklin, 1999; Leichter, 1984; Taylor, 1983; Taylor & Dorsey-Gaines, 1988). At the same time, children from different families have been shown to engage in different types and levels of literacy experiences (Heibert, 1980; Teale, 1986), providing them with different understandings of word and language functions (Heath, 1983; Purcell-Gates, 1996). These findings have contributed to the understanding that children arrive at school with different knowledge and skill levels as well as different understandings about education.

Still, despite existing differences on the first day of school, all students are more likely to experience academic success if they have a supportive home environment. Studies on family involvement during the K–12 school years have concluded that students' home environments and family involvement are important predictors of a variety of academic and nonacademic outcomes (Henderson & Mapp, 2002; Ho & Willms, 1996; Jordan, Orozco, & Averett, 2001; McNeal, 1999; Reynolds & Walberg, 1992). In this chapter, we describe the studies showing the effects of family involvement on student outcomes. First, we summarize the extensive literature showing the effects of family involvement on students' literacy development and reading. We then describe the more limited research on family involvement and students' mathematics and science achievement as well as their school attendance, behavior, attitudes, and adjustment.

PARTNERSHIPS AND ACADEMIC OUTCOMES

Effects on Literacy Development and Reading

Research provides overwhelming evidence of the connection between literacy resources at home and children's literacy development. According to the U.S. Department of Education (Donahue, Finnegan, Lutkus, Allen, & Campbell, 2001), children from homes with more books and more reading by parents tend to perform higher on reading achievement tests than children from less reading-rich environments. Because so much research has looked at how family involvement affects children's literacy development, it is beyond the scope of this chapter to present a full review. Instead, we provide a brief overview of the research, organized according to children's age and grade level.

The Preschool Years

Most preschools provide reading and language experiences to help all students become "ready" for school, and many preschool programs include efforts to involve families with children in literacy activities. Two experimental studies conducted with families of preschool children in Early Head Start (a federal program for infants and toddlers in families with very low income) and Project EASE (Early Access to Success in Education) in Minnesota found that parents could be assisted to work with their children on literacy skills and book-related activities. Both intervention projects found that children in the treatment groups improved their pre-reading language skills compared to students in the control groups (Mathematica, 2001). The programs increased parents' reading stories to children, reading at bedtime, and other reading and language-related activities. A study of the HIPPY (Home Instruction Program for Preschool Youngsters) intervention to increase mothers' reading aloud and working with children on literacy skills came to the same conclusion (Baker, Piotrkowski, & Brooks-Gunn, 1998).

Storybook Reading. Parent-child storybook reading is one of the most studied types of parent involvement in literacy. Storybook reading is also one of the most commonly encouraged forms of parent involvement by teachers and schools. In their review of thirty years of research on the impact of reading to preschool students, Scarborough and Dobrich (1994) concluded that there is a modest impact of shared storybook reading on students' literacy development due mainly to the *quality* of that interaction.

Parent training workshops are a common strategy educators use to help parents improve the quality of their storybook reading with young children. In a study of the effects of parent participation in reading workshops, Jordan, Snow, and Porche (2000) compared the early literacy skills of about 250 kindergarten students whose parents received training versus those who did not. Parents receiving training were taught ways to increase the frequency and quality of parent-child verbal interactions and how to conduct structured activities provided by their child's teacher. Students whose parents were in the training group showed significantly greater improvement on early literacy tests of vocabulary, comprehension, story sequencing, and sound awareness.

Interventions focused on parents with low incomes and limited formal schooling have demonstrated similar results. Lonigan and Whitehurst (1998) compared the effects of a shared reading intervention on preschool children's early literacy skills. Students were randomly assigned to the following groups: (1) teachers reading to a small group of children, (2) parents reading to their children at home, (3) combined teachers and parents reading to children, and (4) a control group of children who received no special intervention. In this study, students who had shared either reading with a parent, small group reading with a teacher, or a combination of the two performed better on reading assessments than did students who experienced no shared reading experiences. In addition, children whose parents were involved in shared reading activities (either solely or in combination with teachers in small group reading) had higher vocabulary levels and oral language use than did children in the teacher-only group.

The results of studies of parent training workshops are important because they show that parents who are assisted to be effectively involved in reading-related activities conduct more and better literacy-focused interactions and that these interactions improve students' reading and literacy skills (see also Faires, Nichols, & Rickelman, 2000; Leslie & Allen, 1999; Phillips, Norris, & Mason, 1996). In particular, Lonigan and Whitehurst's (1998) study provides strong evidence that parents with low incomes and less formal education, who may have weaker reading skills than more economically advantaged parents, can effectively support their children's reading and education.

The Primary Grades

Children's entry to formal schooling marks an important transition in learning and development. The transition to elementary school also has important consequences for parents' roles in their children's literacy

development. Although schools and teachers become significant influences on children's learning to read, the transition to elementary school
does not mean that parents cease to influence their children's reading and
literacy development. Purcell-Gates (1996), for example, found that in
some low-income families, parent involvement in reading *increased* after
their children began formal schooling.

Storybook Reading. Storybook reading continues to be an important
activity for children after they have entered the primary grades. Studies
suggest that there are long-term, multifaceted effects of parent-child
storybook reading on children's language development (Sénéchal &
LeFevre, 2002; Sénéchal, LeFevre, Thomas, & Daley, 1998). In one study,
first-grade children whose parents read more storybooks to them during
the preschool years (*informal* literacy activities) tended to score higher on
vocabulary and listening comprehension assessments. Children whose
parents used books more often to teach letters and words (*formal* literacy
activities) tended to score higher on emergent literacy skills such as
alphabet knowledge, decoding, and invented spelling. These studies
showed that, over time, emergent literacy skills predicted children's reading achievement at the end of first grade, whereas receptive language
skills (i.e., vocabulary and comprehension) predicted reading achievement in the third grade. The complex results are consistent with other
studies indicating that parental involvement with children on varied
reading-related activities helps students develop a number of literacy
skills important for later reading achievement. Moreover, the findings
suggest that parents should be guided to engage young children in a
variety of literacy activities.

Literacy activities experienced at home by children from middle- and
upper-income families may more closely match the school culture than
activities experienced by students from low-income or minority families
(Cairney & Rouge, 1997; Heath, 1983). Based on her research about literacy
classroom practices with low-income children, McCarthey (1999) suggested that teachers establish and maintain frequent and reciprocal communications with all families. She argued that, by developing a better
understanding of children's families and by helping them understand and
use reading resources with their children, teachers will increase home-
school congruence and continuity for all students.

In addition to training workshops to improve parents' skills, other
interventions designed to help teachers incorporate families in their classrooms and in students' reading experiences have proven effective with
culturally diverse families. Paratore et al. (1999) trained low-income
parents who had immigrated to the United States to observe and become
involved in their elementary schoolchildren's literacy activities at home, to
construct portfolios of their children's literacy activities at home, and to
bring these portfolios to parent-teacher conferences. The researchers also
trained teachers to understand family literacy, how to collaborate with

families, and how to use a family literacy portfolio to communicate with their students' parents. Her analyses showed that, during conferences with their children's teachers, parents who developed literacy portfolios with their children at home talked more and provided teachers with more information about their children's literacy activities at home.

Reading Volunteers. Schools often try to bring parent and community volunteers into elementary schools to help children develop literacy skills. Wasik (1998) reviewed empirical research on more than ten adult volunteer programs focused on helping students learn to read. She identified four common features in these programs: (1) a coordinator with knowledge about reading and reading instruction; (2) structured activities for volunteer tutors to use with students; (3) training for the volunteer tutors; and, unexpectedly, (4) poor coordination between tutoring activities and the classroom curriculum. Wasik concluded that these characteristics require evaluation to understand their individual and collective impact on students' literacy development.

In response to Wasik's review, Baker, Gersten, and Keating (2000) evaluated the longitudinal effects of a low-cost community volunteer program on students' reading achievement. After randomly assigning first-grade students to either two years of one-on-one tutoring or a control group, the researchers compared differences in reading achievement at the end of the first and second grades. Students in the tutoring program at the end of second grade had significantly higher oral reading and word comprehension skills than did peers not in the tutoring program. Similarly, Fitzgerald (2001) found that the use of college students as volunteer reading tutors had the potential to improve students' reading outcomes. These studies suggest that community involvement strategies can also have a positive impact on students' reading achievement.

Upper Elementary Grades

Most research on parent involvement and students' reading and literacy skills has been conducted with families of young children in preschool and the primary grades. After the third grade, parents report less involvement in their children's education (Dauber & Epstein, 1993; Eccles & Harold, 1996), and educators report fewer efforts to include parents in their children's schooling (Chen, 2001; Epstein & Dauber, 1991).

A few studies, however, provide important information about the effects of family involvement on the literacy skills and reading achievement of older children. For example, a study of third- and fifth-grade students in an urban school district found that, controlling for prior reading achievement, students in classrooms with teachers who more frequently involved families in learning activities at home had higher gains in reading achievement from one year to the next than did students in other teachers' classrooms (Epstein, 1991, 2001). The data did not identify the specific practices teachers used to involve parents in children's reading, but follow-up interviews with teachers, parents, and administrators in the schools indicated that most involvement activities focused on reading and reading-related activities.

Other intervention studies underscore the importance of family involvement in literacy activities to improve students' reading skills. Shaver and Walls (1998) reported that workshops for parents of students from second through eighth grade promoted families' involvement with children on reading learning packets. As a result, students increased their reading comprehension skills and total reading scores. Also, a study of seventy-one Title I schools in eighteen school districts found that outreach to parents on several types of involvement, including materials on how to help students with reading at home, improved reading achievement over time as students moved from third to fifth grade (Westat and Policy Studies Associates, 2001). The authors reported that gains in test scores between grades 3 and 5 were 50 percent higher for students whose teachers and schools reported high levels of parent outreach in the early grades.

Secondary School

Studies are accumulating that indicate that family and community involvement has a positive influence on student achievement and other measures of success through high school (Catsambis, 2001; Simon, 2001). It is still rare, however, for secondary schools to have well-designed interventions to assist families in interacting with their teens on homework or coursework in specific subjects (Sanders & Epstein, 2000a). Family and community involvement is largely absent from discussions about adolescent literacy and how to teach reading to middle school and high school students. Older students with weak reading skills are often given remedial instruction in vocabulary, comprehension, and writing skills, but little attention is given to the role that family or community reinforcement, interaction, and support might play in encouraging students to master reading competencies (Greenleaf, Schoenbach, Cziko, & Mueller, 2001). Research with a nationally representative sample of secondary students shows that, after controlling for prior levels of achievement, students tend to score higher on reading achievement tests and/or earn higher grades in English if their parents have discussions with them about school and their future plans, check their homework, and maintain high educational expectations (Desimone, 1999; Ho & Willms, 1996; Keith, 1991; Keith et al., 1998; Lee & Croninger, 1994; Simon, 2001). These studies suggest that parent interest in and support for reading may play an important role in adolescents' academic development.

Other studies report that high schools' communications with families are associated with higher levels of students' reading achievement. Controlling for prior achievement, schools that communicated more often with students' families tended to have students who gained more on their reading achievement tests than did schools that did not maintain strong communication practices (Parcel & Dufur, 2001). Parcel and Dufur's work suggests that, if schools establish frequent, positive, and purposeful communications, more parents may be able to provide their children with support for learning that is more closely coordinated with the teachers' goals and that will translate into improved student learning. Clear and helpful communications are essential in secondary schools where parents often feel less confident about their abilities to help adolescents with more advanced curricular activities.

One intervention has been designed to increase family involvement with students on language arts homework in the middle grades. An evaluation of TIPS-Language Arts included 683 students in grades 6 and 8 in two urban middle schools where over 70 percent of the students qualified for free or reduced-price lunch (Epstein, Simon, & Salinas, 1997). The students shared writing prompts, ideas, and drafts of stories and essays, and conducted "family surveys" to discuss their family partners' experiences. Analyses statistically controlled for parent education, student grade level, attendance, fall report card grades, and fall writing sample scores to identify the effects of TIPS interactive homework on students' writing skills in the winter and spring. Students who completed more TIPS homework assignments had higher language arts report card grades. When parents participated, students improved their writing scores from fall to winter and from winter to spring, regardless of their initial abilities.

Effects in Mathematics

Like reading, math is a core subject in schools. This subject matter, however, presents some unique challenges for school, family, and community partnerships. The progressively difficult designs of most mathematics curricula, as well as many parents' own fear of and lack of confidence with the subject matter (Gal & Stoudt, 1995), make it especially important for schools to implement strong partnership programs and activities. Efforts to develop school, family, and community partnerships in math, unfortunately, are relatively rare.

In their review of research on the effects of different types of math interventions, Baker, Gersten, and Lee (2002) found that few programs sought to connect or communicate with students' families, and that when they did, the practices were an "add on" to the program. This failure to incorporate family involvement into mathematics is counter to the findings of much research suggesting that efforts to involve families and community members in students' math learning can improve student performance in that subject.

School-family partnerships are important in math because parents socialize their children in ways that significantly affect their children's self-perceptions of ability and achievement in math. Studies have shown that children's self-concepts of math ability are more closely related to their parents' perceptions of the child's ability than to the actual grades earned (Frome & Eccles, 1998; Parsons, Adler, & Kaczala, 1982). These results are important given evidence demonstrating that children's self-perceptions come to shape their later career decisions (Bleeker & Jacobs, 2004). Schools need to help parents understand when their children are struggling and when their children are excelling in math so that the appropriate encouragement and support can be provided. With this type of parental support, more children will be able to progress further in mathematics.

In addition to shaping children's self-perceptions of math ability, studies show that parental involvement influences children's math achievement. Across all racial groups, students performed better and continued further in mathematics if they participated in parent-child discussions about school and if their parents were active volunteers at the school or members of the PTA or PTO (Catsambis, 2001; Desimone, 1999; Ho & Willms, 1996; Ma, 1999; Valadez, 2002). Also, across racial and ethnic groups, higher parental expectations for their children tended to predict higher math achievement (Hong & Ho, 2005; Yan & Lin, 2005). Using a variety of math outcomes, as well as a wide variety of parent-child interactions, studies clearly demonstrate that families have a strong influence on students' math achievement.

There also is ample evidence that families need help interacting with their children around math. Lerner and Shumow (1997), for example, found that parents tend to believe in the value of more progressive instructional strategies in math (i.e., making children talk about their math work and learning from mistakes) but provide help that is directive and offers few opportunities for students to discover solutions to math problems on their own. Similarly, Hyde and colleagues (Hyde, Else-Quest, Alibali, Knuth, & Romberg, 2006) found significant variation in the ability of mothers to help their children with math homework. In both cases, the researchers concluded that school-family partnerships are needed to help all families understand how to interact with their children on math homework in ways that provide children support and encouragement for learning math.

One effective strategy in this regard has been teachers' use of interactive homework. Balli, Demo, and Wedman (1998), looking at the effect of assigning homework requiring parent-child interactions, found that students receiving this type of homework reported more parent involvement in math. Also, Sheldon and Epstein (2005) found that schools assigning interactive homework in math experienced greater improvement in the percentage of students scoring at or above proficient on standardized math tests than schools that did not assign this type of homework.

Perhaps the strongest evidence to support assigning interactive homework in math has come from Van Voorhis (2007), who used a quasi-experimental design to compare the math achievement of students in classrooms where teachers assigned interactive math homework (treatment) to the achievement of students in classrooms where the teacher did not (control). She found significant differences between students and families in the treatment and control groups. Students assigned interactive math homework reported greater family involvement in math, as well as higher levels of achievement, compared to students in the control condition. This study provides some of the best evidence that teachers can help all families support students' learning in math, and that this support may translate into higher levels of student math achievement.

Other research suggests that schools can improve their students' math achievement by developing a school climate that is welcoming and has the support of the parent community. School climate—the tone or atmosphere of a school—has been associated with leadership style, sense of community, expectations for students, an ethos of caring, and a variety of student outcomes (Goddard, Sweetland, & Hoy, 2000; Gottfredson, Gottfredson, Payne, & Gottfredson, 2005; National Research Council, 2003; Sweetland & Hoy, 2000). Studies show that a more positive school climate exists in schools that are more welcoming to parents and community partners (Desimone, Finn-Stevenson, & Henrich, 2000; Griffith, 1998; Haynes, Comer, & Hamilton-Lee, 1989). Schools with a stronger partnership climate experience higher levels of achievement on standardized math tests, after controlling for prior levels of math achievement and poverty (Sheldon, Epstein, & Galindo, in press). Taken together, the research on math achievement shows that families influence students' attitudes about math and their desire to succeed in math. It also demonstrates that school strategies to help structure parent-child interactions around math and positive school climates that include strong home-school connections can result in improved student performance in mathematics.

Effects in Science

Compared to reading and mathematics, there is far less research about the effects of school, family, and community partnerships on science achievement. Given the current interest in student achievement on science tests, however, it is important to understand findings from the few studies that examine the effects of family and community involvement on students' science achievement.

Family involvement may be especially important for students most at-risk of failure in the area of science. In a national study, Von Secker (2004) found that students from low-income families tended to perform less well in science than their more affluent peers. More important, however, she found that factors such as parent education and home environment helped compensate for the risk of low science achievement associated with lower family income. Finally, Von Secker found that, without these family resources, students from low-income families are likely to see the achievement gap between them and more affluent students widen as they move from fourth to twelfth grade.

Like math, the benefits of family involvement on students' science achievement may occur through the development of positive attitudes about science. George and Kaplan (1998) found that parents play an important role in the development of children's science attitudes through their engagement with science activities and by taking their children to libraries and museums. In perhaps the only study to assess teacher efforts to increase parent-child interactions around science, Van Voorhis (2003) used a quasi-experimental design to test the effects of interactive science homework on parent involvement in science and students' science achievement. She found that families who received weekly interactive homework in science tended to be more involved in science, and students in these families tended to have higher grades in science compared to students whose teachers did not assign the interactive homework. These findings suggest that schools can help more students experience higher achievement in science by encouraging more science-focused family involvement at home.

PARTNERSHIPS AND NONACADEMIC OUTCOMES

Student Attendance

Improving student attendance is an important goal for schools because being at school provides children greater opportunities to learn. A key to improving student attendance at school is using a holistic approach that addresses school and classroom factors, as well as factors related to students' families and communities (Sheldon, 2007). Although most schools have not collaborated systematically with families to reduce student absenteeism, home-school connections are recognized as an important strategy to increase student attendance (Cimmarusti, James, Simpson, & Wright, 1984; Corville-Smith, Ryan, Adams, & Dalicandro, 1998; Epstein & Sheldon, 2002; Weinberg & Weinberg, 1992; Ziesemer, 1984). This approach to improving student attendance is based on research identifying specific parental behaviors such as monitoring students' whereabouts, parent-child discussions about school, volunteering at school, and PTA/PTO membership as important predictors of lower levels of truancy among students (Astone & McLanahan, 1991; Duckworth & DeJung, 1989; McNeal, 1999).

Previous research found that several school partnership practices were associated with student attendance, including communicating with families about student attendance, providing families information about people to contact at school, conducting workshops on attendance, and providing afterschool programs for students (Epstein & Sheldon, 2002). That study suggested that student attendance would improve if schools took a comprehensive approach by implementing activities that support good attendance, by conducting effective home-school connections, and by remaining focused on the goal of improving and maintaining student attendance.

In a follow-up study with a larger and more diverse sample, Sheldon and Epstein (2005) found a reduction in chronic absenteeism associated with the use of communication strategies to inform parents of their children's attendance, as well as the implementation of a partnership program using a diverse set of partnership strategies and activities. The association between school-family communications and reduced absenteeism is consistent with other studies that found that phone calls to parents of absent students are associated with improved student attendance (Helm & Burkett, 1989; Licht, Gard, & Guardino, 1991). Also, providing timely information to families about attendance helped improve attendance rates in high schools (Roderick et al., 1997). Keeping parents informed of their children's attendance at school allows parents to monitor and supervise their children more effectively.

Effects on Student Behavior

Children's behavior, whether in school or out, is related to their home environment and family dynamics. Two decades ago, in their review of the literature, Snyder and Patterson (1987) concluded that certain parenting styles, disciplinary approaches, parental monitoring, family problem-solving strategies, and levels of conflict within the home are all predictive of delinquency among juveniles. Furthermore, they found that the association between sociodemographic characteristics and delinquency is greatly reduced or disappears when these types of family interaction patterns are statistically accounted for. More recently, Davalos, Chavex, and Guardiola (2005) showed that family communication patterns and parental supports of schooling are associated with lower levels of delinquency in secondary students, regardless of ethnicity. Analyzing data from a large national database, Domina (2005) concluded that parental involvement activities reduce behavioral problems and that the favorable effects on student behavior are higher for children from low-income families than for those from high-income families. Many educators understand the relationship between students' family life and school behavior, and many schools include improved student behavior as an important goal and focus of their partnership program efforts.

In addition to improving student behavior at school, implementing partnership practices focused on student behavior also may help improve academic achievement. In a study of 827 African American eighth graders, Sanders (1998) found that student perceptions of family support for school achievement positively influence students' school behavior, which, in turn, has a positive and significant influence on their school grades. Other studies have also demonstrated that students with more parent involvement behave better in school and that school behavior helps predict academic achievement over time (Beyers, Bates, Pettit, & Dodge, 2003; Hill et al., 2004).

Unlike many of the other student outcomes discussed in this chapter, the connection between student behavior and the community context has been understood for a long time. Many have argued that the social and cultural organization of neighborhoods shapes the socialization processes of families and schools (Elliott et al., 1996; Wilson, 1987). Adolescents' exposure to violence in the community, for example, is associated with poor school attendance, low grades, and problem behavior in school (Bowen & Bowen, 1999; Bowen, Bowen, & Ware, 2002). The impact of communities, however, is not always negative. School-community collaborations such as mentoring, safety patrols, and business partnerships may improve school programs and affect student achievement, behavior, and attitudes toward school (McPartland & Nettles, 1991; Nettles, 1991; Sanders, 2001; Sanders & Harvey, 2002).

Although many have suggested that school, family, and community resources could help reduce problem behavior and improve learning in school (Adelman & Taylor, 1998; Epstein, 1995; Noguera, 1995; Sanders, 1998; Taylor & Adelman, 2000), most interventions to improve student behavior have focused on what educators need to do in school to ensure a safe environment. Parents have been given only modest roles in helping to improve student behavior, such as being asked to reinforce school programs (e.g., Gottfredson, Gottfredson, & Hybl, 1993), despite evidence that families and community partners can help schools become safer and more focused on student learning. A study of elementary school students, for example, found that school social workers who helped families and schools communicate with one another improved students' behavior and academic skills (Bowen, 1999). Others have shown that higher levels of family involvement (e.g., attending workshops, volunteering at the school, helping with homework, and being involved with school policy reviews and revisions) are associated with better behavior for middle and high school students (Ma, 2001; Simon, 2001). Also, Sheldon and Epstein (2002) found that schools with improved programs of school, family, and community partnerships reported decreases in the percentages of students sent to the principal, given detentions, and given in-school suspensions. They also found that the implementation of activities to increase parent volunteering and support parenting practices was associated with lower levels of disciplinary actions taken in schools. All of these findings highlight the importance of developing school, family, and community partnership programs to improve students' school behavior.

Effects on Student Attitudes and Adjustment

Family involvement also plays an important role in students' social-emotional development. Students whose parents and family members are more involved in their schooling have been shown to have higher levels of school engagement and achievement motivation (Gonzales-DeHass, Willems, &

Holbein, 2005; Simons-Morton & Crump, 2003). In some cases, students' motivation was shown to mediate the effect of parent involvement on academic achievement (Marchant, Paulson, & Rothlisberg, 2001). In addition, Sanders and Herting (2000) found that family and church support were positively associated with African American adolescents' academic self-concept, which, in turn, was positively related to these students' academic achievement. Family involvement, therefore, may affect achievement through its impact on the development of students' attitudes about and engagement with school, as well as students' perceptions of their academic potential.

These benefits may be most notable during times when children transition to new schools. Studies show that students more successfully transitioned into middle school and high school, measured by grades and test scores, when they had family members who more frequently discussed and monitored their schoolwork (Falbo, Lein, & Amador, 2001; Grolnick, Kurowski, Dunlap, & Hevey, 2000; Gutman & Midgley, 2000). Also, Schulting, Malone, and Dodge (2005) found that, controlling for prior achievement and family background, kindergartners in schools that implemented activities designed to promote family involvement had higher achievement than those in schools that did not conduct this type of partnership outreach.

WHY THIS MATTERS FOR PRINCIPALS

The importance of families has been shown in relation to children's and adolescents' academic and nonacademic school outcomes and is acknowledged in both educational policy and standards for professional educational practice. The wide range of benefits to students that result from family involvement makes partnership outreach a necessary part of how we should define the responsibilities of educators. Nearly all parents want their children to succeed in school and want to help them realize that success (Lareau, 2000; Mapp, 2002). However, because many families face significant barriers to involvement that arise from job constraints, time and income limitations, limited knowledge of the school system, or language and cultural differences, schools need to adopt an organized approach to school, family, and community partnerships that explicitly addresses these challenges.

Studies show that when schools organize involvement activities that specifically address these and other partnership challenges more families are involved in their children's schooling (Simon, 2004; Sheldon & Van Voorhis, 2004). In one study, Epstein and Dauber (1991) showed that the association between family income and involvement disappeared once school outreach was taken into account. Together these studies suggest that more families are likely to be more involved in their children's education if schools provide them with greater partnership opportunities, support, and information.

Schools, therefore, should develop strategic and comprehensive partnership programs to facilitate the academic achievement of all students. Principals are essential to this process and need to lead their staff in reaching out and working with students' families and communities. Through principal leadership, schools can develop strong programs of school, family, and community partnerships and create and sustain cultures of academic achievement and success. In the following chapter, we discuss schools as community organizations and the role of principals in building partnership programs that support students' well-being and school success.

Action Steps for School Leaders

✓ Understand federal, state, and local policies on family and community involvement.

✓ Develop a critical understanding of research on family and community involvement.

✓ Create opportunities for faculty and staff to examine the research on family involvement for important student outcomes and school goals.

REFLECTION QUESTIONS

1. Is the research on school, family, and community partnerships helpful to you as a school leader? Explain.

2. Are most educators knowledgeable about the relationship between family and community involvement and students' school outcomes? Should such information be more broadly shared? If so, what would be the most effective strategies for doing so? What role should school principals play?

3. Are students in your school "successful"? What role does family and community involvement play?

2

*Reculturing Schools
for School, Family, and
Community Partnerships*

In this chapter, we discuss schools as important institutions within their neighborhoods and communities and describe the importance of coordinated school, family, and community partnership programs. We further discuss the role of principals in schools' partnership efforts; obstacles to school, family, and community partnerships; and strategies to address these obstacles.

SCHOOLS AS COMMUNITY INSTITUTIONS

Schools are important institutions within the neighborhoods and communities they serve. Neighborhoods with a variety of strong institutions (e.g., businesses, faith-based institutions, recreation facilities, libraries) are linked to community stability and well-being, as well as a variety of prosocial outcomes for residents. At their best, schools are intricately linked to the community and these outcomes.

One way schools can serve the community is by functioning as a hub for other community resources. Small (2006) found that neighborhood institutions such as schools can act as resource brokers, "organizations possessing ties to businesses, non-profits and government agencies rich in resources" (p. 274). According to Small, through formal and informal interactions, institutional resource brokers can increase neighborhood residents' access to a variety of information and services, such as job training, GED programs, and family counseling. Because of their relative stability and resilience to political and economic shifts, schools are uniquely positioned to act in this capacity.

School personnel can also expand and strengthen children's social networks, which are linked to children's ability to successfully meet the demands of their environments. In addition to teachers and coaches acting as mentors, confidantes, and role models for children, Spilsbury (2005) found that other school personnel also play significant roles. For example, his study in Ohio neighborhoods found that school crossing guards play critical roles within children's social networks. In addition to helping children negotiate busy streets, crossing guards protected children from bullies, provided them with mittens, hats, and scarves during the winter months, buttoned their coats, wiped their noses, and provided emotional support after difficult school days. Other studies (see Sanders, 1996; Stanton-Salazar, 2001) have reported similar findings and underscore the significance of schools and their personnel for students' well-being.

In a study of neighborhoods in Washington, DC, Roman and Moore (2004) found that the presence of strong institutions, such as schools, increased the level of residential engagement in community activities and residents' satisfaction with the block on which they lived. Conversely, the absence of such institutions has been associated with a variety of negative outcomes including high dropout rates from school, violence, crime, and resident isolation (Crowter & South, 2003). Importantly, Roman and Moore (2004) observed that it was not just the presence of strong institutions that mattered. They argued, "Institutions and organizations can be in the neighborhoods, but not of them. In other words, these organizations may have a physical presence, but not necessarily have a social presence with regard to serving neighborhood residents." Thus, to fully actualize their potential to strengthen the social capital and human capital (see Box 2.1) within the neighborhoods and communities they serve, schools must seek to overcome distrust and traditional boundaries and roles to create coordinated programs of school, family, and community partnerships.

Box 2.1   Critical Definitions

Social capital: The interpersonal relationships or network ties that provide access to information and other resources in ways that influence individuals' attitudes, behaviors, and opportunities.

Human capital: Skills and technical knowledge acquired through education and training that can be exchanged for employment and wages in the marketplace.

DEVELOPING A COORDINATED PROGRAM OF SCHOOL, FAMILY, AND COMMUNITY PARTNERSHIPS

Implementing a partnership program in schools can be an effective strategy for getting more students the kind of support linked to their academic success and well-being. The key to having partnership activities reach desired results is to plan and implement them in a coordinated and comprehensive manner. Not all family involvement is the same, and schools need a multidimensional approach to family and community involvement to acknowledge, encourage, and support a range of parental involvement behaviors.

Epstein (1995) identified six types of family and community involvement:

1. Parenting—helping all families understand child and adolescent development and establish home environments that support children as students

2. Communicating—designing and conducting effective two-way communications about school programs and children's progress

3. Volunteering—recruiting and organizing help and support for school programs and student activities

4. Learning at home—providing information and ideas to families about how to help students at home with homework and curricular-related decisions and activities

5. Decision making—including parents in school decisions and developing parent leaders

6. Collaborating with the community—identifying and integrating resources and services from the community to strengthen and support schools, students, and their families

She argues that schools need to develop programs that create involvement across these six types to effectively reach all families and achieve a range of academic and nonacademic goals.

Epstein's call for a multidimensional definition of family involvement has received increasing support in the field of education. More and more, studies are demonstrating that different types of involvement result in different outcomes for children and adolescents (Bertrand & Deslandes, 2005;

Henderson & Mapp, 2002; Jeynes, 2003; Shumow & Miller, 2001). It is thus becoming increasingly clear that educators need to implement a comprehensive range of involvement activities that focus on specific student outcomes as part of a coordinated program of school, family, and community partnerships. As is the case with any type of school reform initiative, the potential for impact rests with the degree to which the initiative is organized and implemented well (Gamse, Millsap, & Goodson, 2002).

Typically, school attempts to involve students' family members and community have occurred through the efforts of individual teachers or staff rather than as a whole-school initiative. When schools create and utilize a programmatic approach to family and community involvement, however, these efforts are more likely to reach all families regardless of family race, ethnicity, or income (Sheldon, 2005). Research examining the development of strong partnership programs has shown that principal leadership, in particular, is vital to their success (Sanders & Harvey, 2002; Sanders & Simon, 2002; Sheldon, 2005; Sheldon & Van Voorhis, 2004; Van Voorhis & Sheldon, 2004).

PRINCIPAL LEADERSHIP AND SCHOOL OUTCOMES

Principals are essential actors in schools and significantly influence whether or not their schools experience academic success. Purkey and Smith (1985), in their review of research on effective schools, found that these studies consistently identified principal leadership as an important characteristic. Fullan (2001) argued that school principals have always been, and are perhaps more so today, critical in determining the fate of any school reform because they can legitimize the program by mobilizing the resources necessary for strong implementation. Without principal leadership, the implementation of any program is not likely to be successful or sustained.

Research on the effects of principal leadership has identified some of the specific ways principals shape their schools. According to Hallinger and Heck (1998), principals affect school outcomes through their influence on four interrelated organizational domains. Specifically, they argue that principals affect a school's purpose and goals, structure and social networks, people, and organizational culture. Each of these domains has been shown to be an important predictor of school outcomes. In setting a school's purpose and goals, the principal frames and conveys a vision for his or her school that affects staff expectations, influences teacher selection and motivation, and increases the likelihood of staff consensus regarding the school's mission.

Principals influence social structures and networks at the school through their effects on interpersonal relationships and on how leadership is exercised. Studies suggest that schools perform better when leadership is more dispersed, with a variety of stakeholders involved in the decision-making process rather than dictated by a single person (Leithwood, 1994; Marks & Printy, 2003). By encouraging mentoring and meetings among colleagues, for example, principals have been shown to positively affect new teachers' experiences and increase their longevity in the profession (Youngs, 2007). Principal leadership that can bring the school community together, generating greater input into the decision-making process and developing networks among individuals throughout the school community, positively affects teachers' professional development and experiences.

The third domain of principal leadership, people, refers to the principal's ability to use his or her interpersonal skills to motivate progressive action in others. These effects are experienced through principals establishing group goals, providing intellectual stimulation and support to staff, providing recognition of success and problems, and transforming the perceptions of school conditions and teachers' commitment to improving the organization (Hallinger & Heck, 1998; Leithwood, 1994). Through the creation of greater social cohesion among members of the school community, principals create stronger, more effective schools.

The fourth domain of school leadership that influences outcomes is the organizational culture. Here theorists argue that principals affect school outcomes by developing shared meanings and values among school personnel (Hallinger & Heck, 1998; Leithwood, 1994; Ogawa & Bossert, 1995). School organizational culture, which is also referred to as school climate, operates as social norms governing people's actions within schools. These norms, according to Youngs (2007), influence teachers and their ability to provide strong instruction to students. School norms also can influence the success of school, family, and community partnerships.

OBSTACLES TO EFFECTIVE SCHOOL, FAMILY, AND COMMUNITY PARTNERSHIPS

A variety of factors influence the quality of school, family, and community partnerships. Some of these, such as time, energy, skills, and parental role construction, rest with families (Hoover-Dempsey, Walker, & Sandler, 2005; Sheldon, 2002). Other factors, such as age, academic needs, temperament, and disposition, rest with students (Davis-Kean & Eccles, 2005; Eccles & Harold, 1993; McDermott, 2008), and still others, such as experience, resources, and professional knowledge, rest with schools (Epstein, 2001; Hoover-Dempsey, Walker, & Sandler, 2005). While acknowledging the multiplicity of factors that affect school, family, and community partnerships, here we focus on specific school norms. We do so because significant research shows that other factors can be minimized when schools develop cultures that support well-designed partnership activities and programs (Comer, 1993; Epstein, 2001).

As previously described, schools are normative environments; that is, they are governed by norms or patterns of behavior regarded as typical more than by clear rules or guidelines. These collective patterns constitute the school's culture. While culture can differ from school to school or classroom to classroom, there are some observed norms that can be found generally and that influence how schools perform their core responsibilities and respond to change. Here we discuss school norms that can impede effective school, family, and community partnerships.

Two such norms are isolation and autonomy. These often reinforcing norms establish defined boundaries around classrooms and teacher practice (Lortie, 2002). The norms of isolation and autonomy, however, can be extended beyond the role of the teachers to the school as a whole. To maintain their ability to carry out their core functions—effective teaching and learning—schools may rationally feel the need to protect or isolate themselves from outside intruders. This isolation also provides a degree of professional autonomy or independence, which educational leaders and practitioners value (National Center for Education Statistics, 1997).

The norms of isolation and autonomy may have evolved due to the very vulnerable nature of schools to influences beyond their control. When describing this vulnerability, Bob Johnson in *Restructuring Schools for Collaboration* (1998) wrote:

> As public institutions supported by tax dollars, schools are accountable to the public and are vulnerable to the demands, supports, and influences of the environment. Not only does the public have a right to raise questions and concerns about schools, but the majority of citizens are themselves products of the public school system. As products of this system, many citizens have definite ideas about what constitutes effective schools and teaching. . . . Unlike organizations such as hospitals, high-tech engineering firms, and Wall Street investment companies, which have their own esoteric language, techniques, and modes of operation, schools lack an organizational mystique. (p. 20)

Thus, these norms are not irrational given that organizational members (e.g., principals and professional educators) are ultimately seen as responsible for carrying out the core responsibilities of schools. Nevertheless, isolation and retreat do not lead to schools of excellence. In fact, these norms have constrained several important collaborative educational initiatives such as team teaching, site-based management teams, and school, family, and community partnerships.

Closely aligned with the norms of autonomy and isolation are the norms of order and control. Many schools are characterized by a high degree of population density and an unselected and sometimes unwilling population. To carry out their core responsibilities, these schools must coordinate and control student behavior. One measure of school effectiveness and teacher effectiveness is often the extent to which they can maintain acceptable levels of order and control. Dysfunctional schools are often described as having "lost control" of students. Having more individuals involved at the school requires relinquishing some of the control exercised by teachers and school administrators. Consequently, many schools may resist the inclusion of "outsiders" in key organizational planning and activities.

Schools, with time, can develop cultures that challenge norms of isolation, autonomy, and control. However, doing so requires conviction, persistence, and strong leadership. This partly explains why, despite federal and state policies, professional standards, and years of research, of Swap's (1993) four models of school-family interaction (see Box 2.2), the Protective Model and the School-to-Home Transmission Model remain dominant. Neither of these models challenges norms of isolation, autonomy, and control—the first because it reduces interaction, and the second because control of the interaction is in the hands of the school.

Box 2.2 Swap's (1993) Four Models of Home-School Interaction

Protective Model: Schools limit most home-school interaction to reduce conflict between families and educators.

School-to-Home Transmission Model: Schools determine when and how home-school interaction occurs.

Curriculum Enrichment Model: Families and school faculty work collaboratively on curricular activities.

Partnership Model: Families and communities work in partnership to support students' learning in a variety of ways.

The Curriculum Enrichment Model (CEM) and the Partnership Model directly challenge norms of autonomy and control because they require shared planning either in specific curricular areas (in the CEM) or in multiple areas of parenting, communication, volunteering, learning at home, and decision making (in the Partnership Model). The collaboration needed to achieve the goals of these models requires time and resources in environments where both are in short supply. Moreover, like most school improvement initiatives, school, family, and community partnerships require long-term commitment because results such as improved test scores may not be realized immediately. Yet, as research and professional standards in education suggest, the benefits of school, family, and community partnerships—including enhanced student achievement and well-being, more informed, engaged, and supportive families, and better resourced schools with improved climates—outweigh the costs (Epstein et al., 2002; Henderson, Mapp, Johnson, & Davies, 2007).

STEPS TOWARD RECULTURED SCHOOLS

Principals can "reculture" their schools to create normative environments that support and nurture partnerships by (1) helping professional educators, families, and community members address and manage issues of power; (2) assisting key stakeholders in building trusting relationships; (3) creating two-way systems of communication and managing conflict; (4) developing volunteer opportunities; and (5) identifying and supporting effective partnership teams. We discuss each in turn.

Addressing Issues of Power

Issues of power within the context of school, family, and community partnerships have not received enough attention but are crucial in the creation of a partnership culture in schools. Fine (1993) criticized the conspicuous absence of discussions of power in the literature on school, family, and community partnerships. In a review of three parental involvement initiatives, she found that issues of power, authority, and control limited the impact of these initiatives to improve educational practices and outcomes for broad populations of students. She concluded:

> The presumption of equality between parents and schools and the refusal to address power struggles has systematically undermined real educational transformation, and has set up parents as well as educators involved with reform. In scenes in which power asymmetries are not addressed and hierarchical bureaucracies are not radically transformed, parents end up looking individually "needy," "naïve," or "hysterical" and appear to be working in opposition to teachers. . . . Rarely do they have the opportunity to work collaboratively with educators inventing what could be a rich, engaging and democratic system for education. (p. 684)

Noguera (1999) also observed that, within urban contexts, greater power is possessed by school authorities than by students' parents and communities due to the unequal distribution of material and nonmaterial resources in the form of financial, political, and social capital; time; and information.

Other examinations of the topic have shown that, even when parents have power, it originates and manifests itself differently from the power that resides with school practitioners. Lake and Billingsley (2000) argued that in public schools parents' power often stems from legislation such as IDEA, whereas schools' and districts' power stems from their positions, control of information, and access to school resources and personnel. Each stakeholder, then, has some power regarding the education of children. The degree of power any individual has differs depending on her or his professional position, social and human capital, and self-efficacy.

How power is used has a great deal to do with the effective implementation of partnership programs. For school, family, and community partnership programs to be successful, all individuals have to understand their power, the source(s) of their power, differences in power, and the most constructive ways to use their power to move partnerships forward and advance the quality of education for all children. In this regard, Warren advocates for the use of relational power. Relational power is the power to achieve goals through collective action, in contrast to unilateral power or achieving goals by exerting dominance over others (see Warren, 2005). Relational power comes from understanding the organizations or people with whom one seeks to work and acting as an equal partner in creating shared visions and addressing critical issues. When principals exercise relational power, they help forge the types of interpersonal relationships and networks necessary for effective school, family, and community partnerships.

Building Trusting Relationships

Trust is an important element of partnerships. Trust is defined as "Firm reliance on the integrity, ability or character of a person or thing" (*American Heritage College Dictionary*, 1993, p. 1451). Trust necessitates the absence of fear about the abuse of power. While understanding the dynamics of power is important, that alone will not move partnerships forward without a concomitant focus on trust and building trusting relationships among families, schools, communities, and students.

Brewster and Railsback (2003) identified several barriers to building and maintaining trusting home-school relationships. These barriers are bad first impressions, poor communication, past experiences, family members' lack of confidence, teachers' lack of confidence, history of discrimination, differing expectations of parent-teacher roles, and lack of confidence in the schools. They recommended that schools interested in building partnerships with diverse families develop strategies that adhere to the following principles of trustworthiness (p. 5):

1. Benevolence—the degree to which the other party takes your best interests to heart and acts to protect them

2. Reliability—the extent to which you can depend upon another party to come through for you, to act consistently, and to follow through

3. Competence—belief in the other party's ability to perform the tasks required by his or her position

4. Honesty—the degree to which the other person or institution demonstrates integrity, represents situations fairly, and speaks truthfully to others

5. Openness—the extent to which the other party welcomes communication and shared information with the people affected

When schools implement practices that honor these principles over time, they are more successful in building trusting relationships with students' families and communities as well as among faculty, staff, and students within the school building.

Bryk and Schneider (2002) also argued that "relational" trust between families and schools is integral to successfully educating students. They described relational trust as emerging from individuals' judgments of others' behaviors in comparison to their beliefs about how they should act. Every interaction between family members and school staff, therefore, is an opportunity to develop or erode trust. According to Bryk and Schneider, relational trust is founded on four criteria that generally correspond to the principles of trustworthiness described previously. First, trust is founded on the respect people have for one another and whether that respect is reciprocated. Next, trust develops based on our judgments that others are competent in their role and that they are able to fulfill their responsibilities. Third, trust develops through individuals' sense that others care and have a sense of regard for them. Finally, trust between families and educators emerges when both parties perceive the other to have integrity and to act in ways consistent with what they say.

Through engaging in trustworthy behaviors, principals as school leaders can motivate and guide other school personnel to do the same. Principals need to demonstrate respect, competence, caring, and integrity with their teachers, staff, students, and students' families. They also need to ensure that school staff demonstrate these same qualities with students, families, and community partners. In doing so, they help create school, family, and community partnerships characterized more by trust and collaboration than distrust and isolation.

Promoting Two-Way Communication and Resolving Conflict

Open communication between home and school has been found to have a positive and significant influence on students' school success (Epstein & Sheldon, 2002; Henderson & Mapp, 2002; Hoover-Dempsey et al., 2005). Indeed, schools regularly communicate with students' families through policy handbooks, newsletters, notes home, school meetings, report cards and progress reports, phone calls, and back-to-school nights (see Box 2.3).

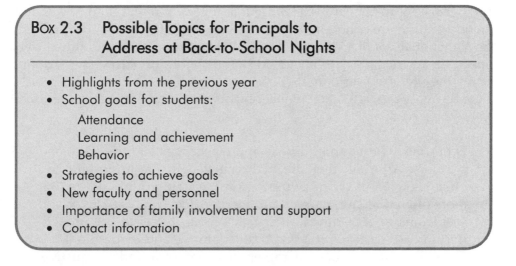

Box 2.3   Possible Topics for Principals to
          Address at Back-to-School Nights

- Highlights from the previous year
- School goals for students:
  - Attendance
  - Learning and achievement
  - Behavior
- Strategies to achieve goals
- New faculty and personnel
- Importance of family involvement and support
- Contact information

However, for home-school communication to be most effective, it should be timely; be focused on school goals, activities, and students' academic progress; and encourage two-way exchange. Two-way communication requires that schools not only send home information for required signatures but that families have a variety of opportunities and formats for asking questions, voicing concerns, gaining additional information, offering insights and suggestions, and extending praise and encouragement.

These opportunities might be formal, for example, parent-teacher and parent-teacher-student conferences, regular office hours with school administrators, parent surveys, and two-way newsletters that provide families the opportunity to respond to newsletter items (see Epstein et al., 2002, and Henderson et al., 2007, for tools and resources). They also might be informal, as in chance encounters when parents drop off students at school or when they are volunteering as chaperones for a field trip or school dance.

With increased interaction and communication between home and school comes the increased possibility of conflict. Conflict between schools and families, in part, stems from their different roles and responsibilities. Parents are focused on and likely to advocate for what is best for their children, not necessarily for what is best for all children within a classroom, grade level, or school. Teachers and administrators, on the other hand, are responsible for identifying practices and making decisions that benefit the larger population of students, not just one child. Conflicts that result from this tension are natural. They are best managed and successfully resolved within the context of a healthy and respectful relationship with appropriate and clearly defined limits and responsibilities for school faculty, staff, and families (Lawrence-Lightfoot, 1978, 2003).

However, conflicts between schools and families also can be dysfunctional. In *Worlds Apart*, Lawrence-Lightfoot (1978) described dysfunctional teacher-parent relationships as those that reflect differences in power and status, resulting in either of the parties' roles being negated or diminished. Dysfunctional conflict, often a result of institutional or individual perspectives and actions that fall outside a framework of partnerships, dominates the literature on parent-teacher relationships. For example, nearly twenty-five years after her pioneering work, Sarah Lawrence-Lightfoot (2003) observed:

> Everyone believes that parents and teachers should be allies and partners. After all, they are both engaged in the important and precious work of raising, guiding, and teaching our children. But more often than not, parents and teachers feel estranged from and suspicious of each other. Their relationship tends to be competitive and adversarial rather than collaborative and empathic. Their encounters feel embattled rather than peaceful and productive. This relational enmity . . . reflects a territorial warfare, a clash of cultures between the two primary arenas of acculturation in our society. (p. xxi)

Swap (1993) suggested general steps to take when conflict occurs. First, the parties involved should promptly discuss the issue. School faculty and staff should be provided professional development on how to share information clearly, listen actively and carefully, and collaboratively define problems and possible solutions to maximize the effectiveness of these discussions. If the conflict cannot be resolved through such exchange, Swap suggested that both parties take time to reflect on and reassess the situation and then reattempt a negotiated definition of the problem and possible solutions. Finally, a neutral mediator, agreed on by both parties, can help resolve the conflict. Through modeling effective communication and conflict management skills, and by providing professional development to faculty and staff, principals can ensure that the school climate is characterized by open and constructive communication that supports students' learning and success.

Supporting Meaningful Volunteerism

Volunteering is a way that families and communities can express the value they place on education and observe children in a school environment to learn how to better help them achieve in school. Schools, students, and teachers also benefit from the work of volunteers. Volunteers can provide students with personal assistance and instruction; reduce the adult-child ratio in classrooms, cafeterias, and on field trips; increase parent participation in school activities and on school committees; decrease teacher workload; increase understanding and awareness of school, district, and state rules and processes; help maintain school equilibrium in the face of high teacher and administrator turnover; share their funds of knowledge with students, faculty, and staff; and create opportunities for the type of informal interaction linked to the development of trusting relationships and greater levels of parental engagement (Brewster & Railsback, 2003; Halsey, 2005; see Box 2.4).

Box 2.4 Eight Reasons for School Volunteers

1. Provide students with one-to-one assistance

2. Reduce the adult-child classroom and school ratio

3. Increase family engagement

4. Decrease teacher workload

5. Increase family awareness of school rules, processes, and needs

6. Help to maintain school equilibrium

7. Share families' cultural knowledge, resources, and experiences

8. Create opportunities for spontaneous, informal home-school interaction

---

The most effective school volunteer programs carry out specific functions (Niemiec, Sikorski, & Walberg, 1999):

1. Recruit volunteers

2. Screen volunteers

3. Train volunteers

4. Monitor volunteer activities

5. Evaluate volunteer activities

6. Show appreciation for volunteers

These functions can be carried out by a full-time volunteer coordinator working alone or preferably with a committee that is part of an active, school-based partnership team. To be most successful, however, these activities must be supported by the school principal. Support can be expressed by securing a room or space for volunteer activities, providing funds for volunteer training, and participating in volunteer appreciation activities and events.

Identifying and Supporting a Partnership Team

Whether a separate structure or a subcommittee of a larger body, such as a school improvement team or leadership council, a team approach has helped many schools build more effective partnerships with their students' families and communities (Comer, 1993; Epstein et al., 2002; Johnson & Ginsberg, 1996). Teams that consist of a school administrator, teacher representatives, parent and community representatives, and other interested stakeholders have several advantages over the more traditional approach of having a single individual responsible for implementing a schoolwide partnership program (Epstein et al., 2002; Sanders & Epstein, 2000b).

First, a team approach allows for multiple and diverse voices to be involved in all stages of partnership program development, from the selection of partnership goals and foci to the evaluation of partnership practices. Parents and community members can offer perspectives to educators that add to their understanding of the students with whom they work. These insights, coupled with educators' professional insights and knowledge, can help all parties develop a more holistic view of the needs and talents of students (Comer & Haynes, 1991). This approach not only increases the likelihood of shared ownership, which is vital for partnership program success, but it helps challenge stereotypical views and perceptions that can hinder collaborative efforts to improve student learning (Burch, Palanki, & Davies, 1995).

Second, because the work of building a partnership program is shared, a team approach reduces the responsibilities of each individual member and, consequently, the likelihood of individual burnout. Furthermore, because a team structure can remain constant even as members change, a team approach increases the likelihood that partnerships will become a permanent part of a school's overall improvement program.

An active and engaged partnership team has been identified as an important factor in the overall quality of partnership programs in elementary, middle, and high schools. Such partnership teams, along with widespread support for partnerships and an adequate level of funding for partnership activities, were found to have a positive and significant influence on family and community engagement regardless of school level or location in an urban or nonurban context (Sanders & Simon, 2002). Principals have been found to play a critical role in the success of partnership teams, often by acting as team "coach." In sports, the coach, though not responsible for running plays or actively participating in a game, is still vital to a team's effective functioning. The role of the principal, like that of a coach, can be to guide, channel, and encourage the partnership team's performance.

The principal of Urban High,[1] a former elementary and middle school coach, exemplified this leadership role (see Sanders & Lewis, 2004). Although she did not always attend partnership team meetings,

---

[1]Urban High is a fictional name given to an NNPS high school that participated in a case study on school, family, and community partnerships (see Sanders & Lewis, 2004, for the full study).

she assigned an assistant administrator to do so and was fully aware and supportive of the team's efforts. She explained:

> Basically, I have an assistant principal that attends the team meetings. She keeps me abreast of activities, because I can't attend all the meetings. She is there on my behalf and she will share everything with me that they are discussing. . . . I am a facilitator. . . . I don't block anything that they are trying to do as long as it makes sense. I want them to generate more community and parent involvement. I want them to know that they have my support with what they are doing. (p. 91)

The principal attended most partnership activities. For example, she was an important presence at the high school's Family Night for Fun and Learning, congenial and engaged with faculty, staff, and parents. She also provided advice on current and future activities, as well as resources that the partnership team needed to enhance its effectiveness such as identifying a large storage room as a site for the parent resource room. Once cleaned, painted, and furnished with a table and chairs, the parent resource room became a focal area for family and community meetings and volunteer activities. In the following passage, Urban High's partnership team co-chair described the importance of this gesture:

> That meeting room is a big deal because I can't think of any other high school that has a designated area for parents and the community to meet. That was a real commitment on her [the principal's] behalf and especially because . . . we have teachers that are floating [who do not have permanent classrooms]. That's a big deal and it really shows that the administration is in favor of what we are doing. (p. 92)

The metaphor of coach works well to describe the way in which principal support for partnership teams can be expressed. This method is, perhaps, the most viable one for principals in large schools who often have more demands and responsibilities than time.

WHY THIS MATTERS FOR PRINCIPALS

As important institutions within their neighborhoods and communities, schools can play a central role in strengthening the social and human capital available to students and their families. To successfully bring this about, principals must be willing to effect change in their schools by exercising leadership that sets a vision, promotes positive interpersonal relationships, motivates others, and creates school environments that nurture partnerships. We suggest that principals can do so by exercising relational power, building trusting relationships, engaging in two-way communication, effectively managing conflict, encouraging meaningful volunteerism, and supporting a team approach to partnerships.

These actions help establish a context that can support and sustain school, family, and community partnerships that realize important goals for schools, students, families, and communities. To achieve truly equitable and inclusive partnership programs, however, principals and the schools they lead must be aware of and responsive to the needs of diverse students and families. The following section focuses on (1) fathers, (2) families of children with disabilities, (3) families with limited English proficiency, and (4) families living in poverty. As described in the Introduction, these populations may be overlooked in partnership programs but are found in most schools and span all racial and ethnic groups. We discuss how schools can create partnership programs that reach out to these populations and, in so doing, ensure that all families and students, not just those traditionally involved, benefit from school, family, and community collaboration.

Action Steps for School Leaders

✓ Become familiar with community organizations and institutions around the school and help these organizations become more familiar with the school and its mission and goals by sending them school newsletters, flyers, and other information.

✓ Provide front office staff with guidelines on how to greet and treat all families and school visitors.

✓ Identify and train a partnership team to organize a coordinated partnership program at your school. Visit the National Network of Partnership Schools Web site (www.partnershipschools.org) for ideas on how to do so.

✓ Review and redesign school-to-home communications (e.g., newsletters, progress reports, and homework) to include opportunities for family members to communicate back to the school or teachers.

REFLECTION QUESTIONS

1. Would you characterize partnership efforts at your school as a coordinated schoolwide program or as disparate activities implemented by individual teachers? Explain.

2. To what extent do the norms of isolation, autonomy, and control operate in your school? What factors do you believe contribute to their presence or absence?

3. Of the five strategies to "reculture" schools, which do you believe is most needed at your school? Which would be easiest to implement? Which would be most challenging to implement? Explain.

PART II

Responding to Diversity

3

Fathers and School, Family, and Community Partnerships

This chapter describes the importance of fathers and father-figures in children's social, emotional, and intellectual development. While mothers are generally more involved in their children's schooling than fathers, involvement by fathers can be expanded and the quality improved through school outreach. Several such outreach activities are described.

WHY FATHERS MATTER

For the past decade, education researchers and practitioners have focused greater attention on the role of fathers in their children's development. This increased interest in fathers has coincided with an increase in federal and state laws addressing noncustodial fathers' financial responsibilities to their children, as well as changes in men and women's conceptions of fatherhood (Tamis-LeMonda & Cabrera, 2002). As our understanding of fathers and fatherhood continues to evolve, many educators are seeking ways to fully engage a greater percentage of fathers in their children's schooling and academic success.

Despite a wealth of evidence, the role of fathers in children's social, emotional, and intellectual development is often overlooked. When we think about how parenting affects child development, mothers generally receive the credit and blame for children's educational and developmental outcomes. This perception is most likely because mothers tend to spend more time with their children than do fathers (Hofferth, Pleck, Stueve, Bianchi, & Sayer, 2002). Fathers, however, have a unique influence on children, including their interaction with peers (Parke et al., 2002), their attitudes about gender roles and stereotypes (Eccles, Adler, & Kaczala, 1982; Jacobs, 1991), and their school performance (U.S. Department of Education, 1997). To ignore fathers and not include them in the development of family and community involvement activities is to ignore an important resource in children's lives.

One of the first issues one must confront when thinking about involving fathers in children's education relates to who we mean when we use the term *father*. We use *father* here to refer to biological fathers, stepfathers, adopted fathers, as well as nonrelated father-figures in children's lives. This broad definition of father is consistent with research. Amato and Rivera (1999), for example, found that father involvement was associated with lower levels of behavior problems in children, regardless of whether a biological father or stepfather was involved (see also, Marsiglio, Amato, Day, & Lamb, 2000). Students for whom a biological father is not accessible can still benefit from the involvement of a stepfather, adopted father, or father-figure. This means that school outreach to involve fathers should be inclusive of all types of fathers and other important male role models in students' lives.

Given the wealth of research and best practice on school, family, and community partnerships, surprisingly little has been written on the involvement of fathers in children's K–12 education. In this chapter, we begin by presenting some demographic data that describe who the fathers in this country are. Next, we discuss some of the research and programs that have focused on involving fathers in their children's education. Based on this discussion, we recommend strategies for schools and school leaders interested in increasing fathers' involvement in partnership activities. Finally, this chapter presents examples of partnership practices to involve fathers that have been conducted in schools across the United States. These examples are included to provide guidance and inspiration to those interested in fostering greater father involvement in children's schooling.

FATHER DEMOGRAPHICS

According to the national census and other surveys, approximately three-quarters of all children under the age of eighteen live with their biological father, stepfather, adopted father, or some other significant male in their household (Hofferth et al., 2002). This means that most fathers are living in a household where a child is either enrolled in school or approaching school age. These men have the potential to significantly influence the cognitive, social, and emotional development of their sons and daughters.

Through their examination of U.S. Census and other national datasets, Hernandez and Brandon (2002) estimated that fathers living in a household with a child under the age of eighteen were mostly non-Hispanic whites, although this proportion declined from 78 percent in 1990 to 73 percent in 1999. They also found that one in five of these fathers were either foreign-born or married to a woman born outside the United States. Most tended to be older (thirty to forty-nine years old) and were almost always married (95 percent in 1990 and 93 percent in 1999).

Variation among these fathers increased dramatically in regard to levels of educational attainment. Hernandez and Brandon (2002) found that in 1999, 7.6 percent of non-Hispanic white fathers had not completed high school compared to 13.9 percent of non-Hispanic blacks, 23.6 percent of U.S.-born Hispanics, and 54.9 percent of immigrant Hispanic fathers. Much higher rates of non-Hispanic whites (U.S.-born or immigrant) had completed college compared to black or Hispanic (U.S.-born or immigrant) fathers. These differences in educational attainment are important because fathers with more education may have a greater sense of familiarity and comfort with their children's schools. Schools working to increase fathers' involvement need to understand that differences in involvement across racial or ethnic groups may be related to differences in educational attainment, and they should thus develop activities suitable for fathers with diverse educational backgrounds.

The changing nature of family structure in the United States has obvious and important implications for any initiative to involve fathers in children's education. According to a report by the Centers for Disease Control (2002), 49 percent of all cohabitation relationships result in a divorce or separation within five years. This figure increases to nearly 70 percent in communities with high unemployment and low family incomes. Consequently, schools located in central- and inner-city areas are more likely to educate students whose mothers and fathers do not live together and who have experienced some type of dissolution of their relationship.

National statistics also indicate that African American students are more likely to come from households that have experienced some marital disruption. Approximately one-third of all children are raised in households that have experienced at least one divorce or separation (Hofferth et al., 2002). This rate, however, is much higher for African American children (68.3 percent) compared to white and Hispanic children (29.1 percent and 37.1 percent, respectively). For schools located in large urban areas and educating largely African American students, efforts to involve fathers are more likely to confront issues surrounding divorce and marital disruption. These schools may need to devote more effort to involving fathers and increasing the quality of father-child interactions than do schools located in wealthier areas where the divorce rate is likely to be lower and the percentage of resident fathers probably higher.

THE ROLE OF FATHERS

Fathers and Children

Despite the difficulties of involving fathers, current research suggests that these efforts can have positive educational and developmental consequences for children. This section begins with an overview of resident and nonresident fathers' involvement, followed by a summary of research linking fathers' involvement to their children's education and developmental outcomes.

In general, resident fathers tend to be more involved in raising their children than are nonresident fathers, and biological resident fathers are more involved than other types of fathers. Fathers spend most of their time with their children talking and engaging in play. The average amount of time any type of father spends reading with a child is relatively low. The amount of time fathers spend with their children also decreases as children get older and enter adolescence (Hofferth et al., 2002).

The involvement of fathers with their nonresident children presents a more complicated picture. Most nonresident fathers maintain monthly contact with their children. However, one-third reported having no contact with their children in a twelve-month period (Hofferth et al., 2002). Nonresident fathers tend to engage in more fun and leisure activities with their children. Only 16 percent reported spending some time with their children on school-related activities. Thus, while most children spend a significant amount of time in school, few resident and fewer nonresident fathers involve themselves in this aspect of their children's lives.

Fathers' Involvement With Schooling

In one of the first large-scale surveys of fathers' involvement, the U.S. Department of Education found that resident fathers, compared to mothers, are much less likely to be involved at their children's schools (U.S. Department of Education, 1997). According to this report, 25 percent of married, resident fathers reported never participating in a school activity.

For nonresident fathers, this figure was 69 percent. These figures suggest that many fathers do not develop any relationship with their children's schools or teachers. Many fathers living with their children in two-parent households allow home-school relationships to be managed by and through mothers.

Across grade levels, fathers' involvement has important similarities and differences to mothers' involvement. For both mothers and fathers, involvement at school decreases as children grow older (U.S. Department of Education, 1997). The rate of this decline, however, is greater for mothers than it is for fathers. Levels of fathers' involvement decline only slightly once children enter high schools (30 percent in grades K–5 versus 23 percent in grades 9–12), compared to a sharper decline in mothers' involvement at school across these grade levels (68 percent in grades K–5 versus 38 percent in grades 9–12). Thus, the gap between mothers' and fathers' involvement at school appears to decrease as children progress through school.

Differences in observed patterns of involvement over time may be a reflection of variations in the ways mothers and fathers are involved in their children's education. Compared to mothers, fathers are less likely to attend school meetings, such as open houses or PTA meetings, or to volunteer at the school (U.S. Department of Education, 1997). Also, in a recent 2008 report released by the National Center for Fathering (www.fathers.com), 38 percent of fathers indicated they had never read a book to their child. Men, however, are nearly as likely to attend school events such as athletic competitions or school plays. As children age and move through grade levels, mothers are more likely to pull back from their children's schools than are fathers, who are generally less involved to begin with.

One important way fathers affect children's development is through the provision of economic support. Children whose nonresident fathers consistently pay child support tend to have more positive school outcomes, including higher academic achievement, than students whose fathers do not (Menning, 2006; Stewart, 2003). Earlier research, in fact, showed that payment of child support, but not contact or visitation with the nonresident father, predicted more positive child outcomes (King, 1994; Seltzer, 1994). However, the provision of financial support falls short of fully explaining the importance of fathers in children's school success.

For example, Amato and Rivera's (1999) review of the paternal involvement literature found that 80 percent of the sixty-eight studies reviewed reported significant positive relationships between fathers' involvement and child well-being, including fewer behavioral issues and increased student achievement. Similarly, Flouri and Buchanan (2004) examined longitudinal data from a National Child Development Study (NCDS) of some 17,000 children born between March 3 and 9, 1958, in England, Scotland, and Wales. Fathers' involvement and mothers' involvement at age seven independently predicted educational attainment by age twenty. The relationship between parents' involvement and educational attainment was not stronger for sons than for daughters. In addition, growing up in a single-parent household did not weaken the relationship between fathers' involvement or mothers' involvement and educational outcomes.

It has become increasingly clear that fathers' effects on children's education are strongly related to the quality of interactions they have together. Menning (2006) has shown that adolescents whose fathers engage them in discussions about school and academic and nonacademic issues tend to earn higher grades and are significantly more likely to graduate from high school than adolescents without such interactions. He also found that, when father-child discussions are taken into consideration, the amount of time nonresident fathers spend with their children has little to no effect on school outcomes.

The implications of these findings are obvious for schools. Educators do not need to work tirelessly to ensure that all fathers attend every meeting; rather, efforts to involve fathers need to focus on helping these men participate in productive interactions with their children. Especially with regard to nonresident fathers, schools should emphasize to men that they can have a significant positive impact on their children by making the most of the time they have with their sons and daughters.

GUIDELINES FOR DEVELOPING PARTNERSHIP EFFORTS TO INVOLVE FATHERS

The following guidelines and general strategies for involving fathers have been developed by McBride and Rane (1996) in their efforts to increase the involvement of fathers and male role models in children's education. For the purposes of this book, these issues have been organized into four general categories: (1) program design and delivery, (2) staff training and professional development, (3) the role of mothers, and (4) fathers' fears. Principals leading schools to involve more fathers need to consider each of these categories before implementing such activities (see Box 3.1).

Box 3.1   Four Factors to Consider When Involving Fathers

Program Design and Delivery

Careful forethought can go a long way to making your efforts to involve fathers as successful as possible. Begin by developing a vision of what you want fathers and other significant males to do and why you think they are uniquely qualified for some types of participation.

Staff Training and Professional Development

Consider how you will train staff to lead this project to involve fathers and father-figures. Also, consider some of the possible challenges and changes in interpersonal dynamics that might arise as more men become involved.

The Role of Mothers

Include mothers in your efforts to involve men. Mothers are often more involved and can effectively encourage fathers to become involved in children's schooling.

Fathers' Fears

Because many men may initially feel uncomfortable with father involvement activities, expect this initiative to take time to develop. Build on existing successful practices that traditionally have not focused on men.

Program Design and Delivery

When schools begin to plan coordinated activities to engage fathers, they should consider the steps described in the following paragraphs. By following these steps, educators will be able to target their efforts and increase the likelihood of success.

Be Specific About Goals

Before any work to target and involve fathers begins in earnest, educators must clarify specific reasons why they think these efforts are important and can enhance children's educational experience.

Address Resistance to the Initiative

Schools often operate in a context of limited resources. As a result, many people may question whether or not resources should be spent on involving fathers when these same resources can be spent on instruction or even to involve mothers (who are more likely to be engaged in their children's learning). To overcome such resistance, partnership organizers must have a clear and convincing rationale for focusing on fathers that is grounded in the research described in this chapter as well as the specific needs and concerns of their students and families. Partnership organizers, then, need to enlist partnership team members and other parents, teachers, school administrators, and community leaders to help them make the case for devoting resources to increasing fathers' involvement.

Define Fatherhood

Although children growing up in single-mother households may not see their biological fathers on a daily or even weekly basis, they are likely to have some type of male role model or father-figure in their lives. Developing a strong father involvement program will require the inclusion of such father-figures. Focusing solely on biological fathers excludes a large number of men who can play a valuable and significant role in children's education and development.

Begin With Current Practices

Most schools in the United States already do some work to connect with and involve families in children's schooling. In developing an initiative to involve fathers, principals should encourage the partnership leaders at their schools to examine current practices. A valuable first step is to evaluate the existing partnership or school improvement plan and identify which of the current practices can be adapted to be more attractive and responsive to fathers.

Staff Training and Professional Development

Researchers have shown that teachers and administrators receive very little training in partnerships and in how they might establish more positive home-school relationships (Epstein & Sanders, 2006). This is even truer with regard to fathers' involvement. Principals and school districts committed to gaining more support for students from fathers need to consider providing teachers and staff professional development and training on father involvement. Seek out national organizations that can serve as a resource on this topic such as the National Center for Fathers and Families (www. ncoff.gse.upenn.edu), the National Center on Fathering (www.fathers.com), and the National PTA (www.pta.org).

Furthermore, given that more women work in the field of education and are entering the teaching profession at greater rates than are men, and that women are likely to be more involved in their children's education (NCES, 1997), women will probably be leading or playing a significant role in initiatives to involve fathers in schools. To experience the greatest success, these individuals need to be knowledgeable about, and sensitive to, differences in the ways that men and women parent (McBride & Rane, 1997). For example, it has been shown that men and women communicate and interact with children differently, as well as process thoughts and emotions differently. Denying these differences may limit attempts to increase fathers' involvement in their children's education.

The Role of Mothers

Fathers are more likely to be involved in their children's education when the mothers are involved. Because mothers tend to be the primary contact between the school and the children's home, it is important to explain to them why activities focused on fathers' involvement are being implemented. Moreover, mothers should be encouraged to help facilitate fathers' involvement. In the course of getting help from mothers, however, it is important to maintain the regular family involvement initiatives that traditionally involve mothers and fathers together. It also may be important to consider implementing practices that focus specifically on mothers' involvement as well.

Fathers' Fears

Like general partnership programs, school efforts to involve fathers and other males in students' schooling will take time to develop into a high-quality initiative. Epstein and colleagues (2002) suggest that it takes schools three years to develop high-quality programs of school, family, and community partnerships. This may also be a realistic timeline for the development of an effective program to involve men in children's education. More important, perhaps, is the understanding that the development of these programs should progress slowly, building upon early successes with a core group of men likely to respond quickly to invitations for involvement.

Initial efforts to involve more fathers might concentrate on creating a supportive climate of involvement for men. Having activities solely for men will begin to develop a culture of male involvement, allowing more men to feel secure about their role at the school and in their children's schooling. Part of developing this culture is making clear to men the expectation that they should and will be involved in their sons' and daughters' education and development. Strategies to help communicate this expectation include asking for nonresident fathers' names, addresses, and contact information on enrollment forms; on occasion, and when possible, talking to fathers when making calls home; scheduling meetings at school when men are more likely to be able to attend; and letting fathers know that involvement is more than volunteering at the school and can take place at work, in the community, or at home. Finally, communicating the expectation that fathers should be involved in their children's education requires explicitly inviting men to attend and participate in school events and projects.

PRACTICAL PARTNERSHIP ACTIVITIES

As interest grows in involving fathers and father-figures in children's schooling, many schools struggle with understanding the different kinds of activities they might implement. One type of practice schools can easily implement is a family workshop explicitly aimed at getting fathers to read more often with their children. According to the National Center on Fathering, in 1999, 40 percent of fathers had never read a book to their child. This figure improved a mere 2 percent, to 38 percent, according to the most recent survey conducted in 2008. More efforts need to be made to encourage and enable all fathers to read to their children on occasion. The program Fathers Reading Every Day (FRED), implemented at Roosevelt Elementary School in 2007 and sponsored by the Minnesota Humanities Commission, illustrates many important features of a fathers' reading workshop (see Box 3.2).

Box 3.2   Fathers Reading Every Day (FRED)

Roosevelt Elementary School, St. Paul, Minnesota

FRED was popular at Roosevelt Elementary this year. FRED is Fathers Reading Every Day, a program of the Minnesota Humanities Commission that encourages men to read at home and to get more involved in their children's education. At Roosevelt, FRED was a month-long initiative featuring two family reading sessions in December and January, which combined food, storytelling, guest readers, free books and camaraderie. Working with the commission, the school's Action Team for Partnerships (ATP) welcomed FRED and worked hard to make it a successful undertaking. The team even arranged and paid for taxis for families who did not have transportation.

The result was that large groups of men and some single mothers and their school-aged children attended both sessions. Dinner was followed by a storybook reading session. Among the guest readers were the school's custodian, librarian assistant, and a "live" Cat in the Hat. After the reading period, children went to another area for activities and parents had the opportunity to discuss different types of literature and storytelling. They learned more about the Success for All reading program used at the school and received suggestions about reading with their children from a literacy teacher.

The parents also received *What Daddies Do Best*, a book that, when turned over, reads *What Mommies Do Best*. The families saw a great many parents reading with their children. They clearly understood how important they are to their children's education. Parents and children also participated in a choral reading. Before leaving, children selected two free books to take home. Through FRED's influence, students saw their parents show more interest in listening to them read at home, and in reading themselves. Some of the children enjoyed the evening so much that they wanted to know if there would be another "dad thing."

Improving student achievement through reading instruction is one of the school's and the ATP's priorities. Targeting activities to male caregivers was a need that was identified when the school completed the NNPS annual UPDATE evaluation. Although FRED specifies "fathers," the program also welcomed single mothers. Next year, the school will change the name to include both groups. More than 50 parents and 80 children attended the FRED sessions. The school principal endorsed the program in collaboration with the ATP. The team's facilitator ordered food, arranged for taxis and childcare. School staff members and parents volunteered as readers. Teachers developed and supervised activities for the children.

FRED cost about $885, including the food, taxi fares, door prizes and interpreters for Hispanic and Hmong families. Title I funding covered these costs, and the humanities council provided the books. "Because of this program my children remind us to read, even if I'm busy," said one parent. Other participants agreed that the program helped them to become more involved in helping their children read, forging happy memories in the process.

Christine Cardinal, ATP Facilitator, Parent Educator

Source: Maushard, M., Martin, C., Hutchins, D., Greenfeld, M., Thomas, B., Fournier, A., & Pickett, G. (Eds.). (2007). *Promising partnership practices 2007*. Baltimore, MD: National Network of Partnership Schools. Reprinted with permission, © 2007 National Network of Partnership Schools, Johns Hopkins University.

One of the first things that must be considered in planning any family night or workshop is the purpose of the activity. In this case, the overarching goal of FRED was to inform fathers about how they might read with their children and to provide them with resources to facilitate father-child reading at home. Toward this end, the evening workshop included opportunities for fathers to talk with one another about books and storytelling, to learn about children's books that feature fathers, and to practice strategies for reading with children. Another important consideration in planning family nights is to determine how to meet the challenges that make attendance at these activities less likely. In the case of FRED, the organizers offered dinner to attendees, arranged transportation, and provided childcare at the event for families in need of these services. The school also provided translation services for fathers who were not fluent English speakers. By providing these services, the school addressed challenges to fathers' participation and communicated a serious desire to involve *all* fathers in their children's education. In addition to meeting challenges and providing opportunities to learn, father workshops should also provide participants with resources that allow them to use the knowledge gained at the workshop at home. The FRED program provided attendees with books to take home to read with their young children.

Fathers can also be valuable partners in schools' efforts to improve student behavior (see Box 3.3). In Cleveland, Ohio, the Robert H. Jamison School hosted a "Men's Day" to gain the support of fathers and father-figures in improving student attendance and reducing classroom disruptions. The event was held in the morning. Fathers were provided breakfast while community members and school staff talked with them about the importance of being involved in their children's education. The event also provided these fathers the opportunity to meet and speak with their children's teachers.

Box 3.3   Men's Day

Robert H. Jamison School, Cleveland, Ohio

The staff at Robert H. Jamison School had a problem: Suspensions and classroom disruptions were on the rise, and students were missing class and roaming the hallways. Rather than responding with punishments, the administration, led by the Action Team for Partnerships (ATP), tried a positive solution: getting dads and other men important in the students' lives involved. The school hosted Men's Day, inviting fathers, grandfathers, uncles, and other male role models to a special waffle breakfast.

At the breakfast, speakers encouraged the men to volunteer, visit the school during the day, and have conferences with teachers. After breakfast, each man had his picture taken and wrote a note of encouragement to his child or family member. The school posted these words of support with the pictures around the school for the children to see. About twenty-five men attended.

Jamison's ATP planned Men's Day to increase volunteerism and give fathers more ownership in the K–8 school. This strategy worked: Many of the men stayed after the event to help monitor the hallways and keep students in class. Some even organized themselves to help out again the following day.

The breakfast was a joint effort: Community members provided the food, ATP members cooked, and two of the speakers came from the community. Another was from the school staff. The school sent home fliers with students and also e-mailed parents directly to invite them. Getting upper-grade students to take the fliers home was a challenge; the school included response notices with the fliers to ensure that enough families heard about the event.

Since Men's Day, behavior and attendance at Jamison have improved noticeably. Teachers have been able to teach with fewer interruptions. There have been fewer students in "lockout" and more students in the classrooms. Most important, Jamison has strengthened the influence of positive male role models on students, increasing family involvement in the school. Plans for next year include scheduling the activity after school, when more dads will be available.

Doris Wright, Family Liaison

Source: Brownstein, J., Maushard, M., Robinson, J., Greenfeld, M., & Hutchins, D. (Eds.). (2006). *Promising partnership practices 2006.* Baltimore, MD: National Network of Partnership Schools. Reprinted with permission, © 2006 National Network of Partnership Schools, Johns Hopkins University.

This type of activity is not uncommon. Many schools host "Doughnuts for Dads" events. Although this type of partnership activity might seem simple, it can be an important early step in the development of any father involvement initiative. First, these events are explicit in communicating to men that involvement in their children's education is valued. They also help create a context where fathers can meet and discover they are not alone in wanting to help their children succeed in school. Finally, these activities help counter gender role stereotypes, open lines of communication with school staff, and begin the process of generating greater male participation in other partnership activities.

Given that men are less inclined to visit or volunteer at the school, educators may need to consider alternative settings where fathers can interact with their children on school-related projects. For example, the William Cullen Bryant School in Cleveland, Ohio, developed a partnership with a national home improvement warehouse store. The store volunteered to conduct father-child woodworking classes on their premises in the evenings, thus providing fathers who might have been uncomfortable at the school an opportunity to develop more positive relationships with their children in a nonacademic environment. Also, because members of the school PTO coordinated and attended the event, information about other school activities and upcoming family events was directly shared with these fathers (see Box 3.4).

Box 3.4   Fathers Matter

William Cullen Bryant School, Cleveland, Ohio

William Cullen Bryant School partnered with another school to involve fathers and their children in a program offered in the community. Fathers Matter involved monthly woodworking projects for parents and their children at Lowe's Home Improvement. On the last Tuesday of every month from October to May, fathers and their children met at Lowe's from 6:00–7:00 pm to build birdhouses, bird feeders, planters, toolboxes, picture frames, spice racks, and toy trucks. Even though families worked together in a non-academic setting, the projects helped students practice their literacy and math skills in real-world applications.

The family liaisons for both schools met with Lowe's store management. After agreeing to the partnership, the family liaisons created an invitation describing the program to parents. They called parents to manage the number of families attending each month, because a limited number of students from each school could participate. Every month, the liaisons set up a table with school information at Lowe's and helped Lowe's employees clean up after the project. The PTO donated refreshments for the participating parents and their children.

(Continued)

(Continued)

Through Fathers Matter, students worked with their parents on woodworking projects and practiced their literacy and math skills in the real world. Students were particularly excited because they could use their creations at home. Teachers enjoyed seeing fathers and children working together. Parent comments included: "This workshop gives my children and me a chance to spend quality time together," and "My daughter learned that building projects are fun as well as productive." Based on the positive results, William Cullen Bryant hopes to continue their partnership with Lowe's next year.

Laura Gump, Family Liaison

Source: Salinas, K., & Rodriguez-Jansorn, N., with Neuman, B., & Harvey, A. (2003). *Promising partnership practices 2003.* Baltimore, MD: National Network of Partnership Schools. Reprinted with permission, © 2003 National Network of Partnership Schools, Johns Hopkins University.

WHY THIS MATTERS FOR PRINCIPALS

When schools encourage fathers' involvement in their children's schooling, children benefit. Without such encouragement, fathers' involvement is likely to be limited, especially among nonresident fathers and those with low educational attainment. Principal leadership is needed to ensure that outreach to fathers occurs and that it is well planned; informed by research, best practice, and the needs of the school and its families; inclusive of mothers; and responsive to fathers' interests and concerns. When schools conduct such activities as part of schoolwide partnership programs, they send a clear message to fathers that their involvement is needed, desired, and important to children's school success.

Action Steps for School Leaders

✓ Communicate widely and regularly that mothers' *and* fathers' involvement is welcomed and appreciated.

✓ Ensure that the school partnership team implements at least one father-focused partnership activity each year.

✓ Create a volunteer survey with separate optional sections for mothers and fathers.

REFLECTION QUESTIONS

1. How do marriage and divorce trends affect your school's approach to and involvement of fathers? What are some factors that are especially critical to consider when dealing with the involvement of divorced parents?

2. How might you design partnership activities to respond to the fact that many fathers work full-time and may not have the flexibility in their jobs to get involved at the school during school hours?

3. Why do you think fathers are less likely to get involved in their children's schooling than mothers? Given your response, what do you think is the best approach to increasing fathers' involvement in their children's learning?

4

Families of Children With Disabilities and School, Family, and Community Partnerships

Schools intent on reaching the families of all students and maximizing the benefits of family involvement for all children can implement specific strategies that support the involvement of families of children with disabilities. This chapter describes processes and practices all schools can employ to ensure that the families of students with disabilities have the information and support they need to be effective partners in their children's learning and development.

IDEA AND CHILDREN WITH DISABILITIES

Today, over 6 million children and youth in the United States receive special education and related services to meet their learning needs. The most common types of disabilities among students aged six to twenty-one are specific learning disabilities (51 percent), speech and language impairments (19 percent), mental retardation (11 percent), and emotional disturbance (8 percent) (Moles, 2005). The educational opportunities of students with disabilities were drastically changed in 1975 when the U.S. Congress found that "the special educational needs of such children are not being fully met." It passed legislation, which would later become the Individuals With Disabilities Education Act (IDEA), requiring that students with special needs be taught "to the maximum extent appropriate" in the same classrooms with mainstream students (Congress of the United States of America, 1975).

To realize the full promise of this legislation and its subsequent reauthorizations, schools must not only create learning environments that support the individual needs of these diverse learners but also work collaboratively with their families. The importance of involving families in the education of students with disabilities is well documented. Research has shown that students with disabilities whose parents are involved in their education are more successful than similar students whose parents are not involved (Turnbull, Turnbull, Shank, & Leal, 1995). It also is established that the earlier this involvement takes place, the greater the benefits for the child and family (Anastasiow, 1986).

IDEA provided parents the right to examine their children's records, challenge school evaluations, make formal complaints, and pursue due process hearings. But these rights center on procedure, not partnerships. Aside from the information gathered at mandatory Admission, Review, and Dismissal (ARD) and Individual Education Plan (IEP) meetings, the families of many special needs children are often left on their own to figure out how to best support their children as individuals and learners as they progress through school (McDermott, 2008), sometimes without a full understanding of how the special education system operates (Harry, Allen, & McLaughlin, 1995).

DISTRICT AND SCHOOL OUTREACH TO FAMILIES OF CHILDREN WITH DISABILITIES

When Congress renewed IDEA in 1997, it authorized an evaluation of progress toward the goals of the legislation at the state and local levels. Toward that end, the Study of State and Local Implementation and Impact of the Individuals With Disabilities Education Act (SLIIDEA) investigated progress on nine topics, including increasing parent participation in the education of children with disabilities. In 2002–2003, surveys were sent to special education personnel in all fifty states and the District of Columbia, forming a nationally representative sample of 959 districts and 4,448 elementary, middle, and high schools, to examine progress on the IDEA goals (Misra, 2006).

According to the study, almost all the districts surveyed either provided written guidelines on parental involvement for families of children with disabilities or were located in states that provided them. These guidelines concerned a variety of topics, most commonly parents' legal rights under the law, development and implementation of the IEP, and accommodations available for district and statewide assessments. Schools and districts, however, were less likely (fewer than 50 percent) to collect data on parent involvement and to use the data to evaluate outreach and to plan professional development.

Furthermore, only a few schools reported that all or most of their general education teachers participated in professional development activities related to increasing parental engagement. Fewer than 50 percent of schools reported that special educators participated in professional development on increasing parent involvement. The SLIIDEA study did find, however, that the schools most likely to take initiatives to foster greater involvement of families of students with special needs shared several characteristics, including high levels of teacher (both general and special educators) participation in professional development on parent involvement.

Thus, while many schools, districts, and states have taken some actions to increase the involvement of families of children with disabilities, it is evident that more progress is needed. Misra (2006) observed that, "with only one-half of schools reporting that their special education teachers are well prepared to increase parental involvement, and even fewer reporting that general educators are well prepared, there is much room for improvement at the state, district and school levels" (p. 5).

SPECIFIC NEEDS AND EXPERIENCES OF FAMILIES OF CHILDREN WITH DISABILITIES

Although the families of children with disabilities share many of the same concerns and experience the same needs as families with children in general education, they also have unique needs and concerns. According to Burello and Wright (1992),

> Parents tend to experience a sequence of reactions upon learning of their child's special education needs. The feelings are normal but must be validated by the professionals before a healthy adjustment can be realized. Disbelief, guilt, rejection, shame, denial, hopelessness, insecurity and loneliness characterize some parental reactions. A primary goal must be to assist parents in working through their feelings with their child. (p. 8)

In addition to emotional support, families require information in order to understand and provide their children with the resources they need to realize their full potential (McDermott, 2008).

However, some schools have not been successful in providing families of children with disabilities the required supports. For example, in a study of fathers' involvement in their children's special education program, League and Ford (1996) found that many fathers lack the necessary information and feedback from schools to become actively engaged in their children's learning. Fathers in the study reported that information from the school was often sporadic and unclear. They also complained that they were not supported in becoming involved in varied ways in their children's learning at school or at home. These fathers had suggestions for ways that the school could encourage greater father and, ultimately, greater family involvement; however, the fathers did not feel as though they had a vehicle for expressing their concerns or offering suggestions.

Several more recent studies have reported similar findings. Indeed, a survey of parents' satisfaction with their children's schooling found that, while the majority of parents of students with disabilities are at least somewhat satisfied with all aspects of their children's schooling, the percentage who report being dissatisfied is higher than in the general population (Newman, 2005). Moreover, dissatisfaction is higher among families of secondary school students than among families of elementary school students. For example, although 52 percent of parents of young children (six to thirteen years old) with disabilities reported being very satisfied with their children's schools, only 37 percent of parents of older children (thirteen to seventeen years old) with disabilities reported being very satisfied. Parents of similar-age students in the general population were, respectively, 8 and 11 percentage points more likely to report being very satisfied with their children's schools. These trends correspond with research suggesting that the family-school relationship becomes increasingly distant as students move into and through elementary school, and parents develop a growing sense of disillusionment with special education programs (Harry et al., 1995).

Parents' satisfaction with their children's schooling also differs by disability category. The highest levels of satisfaction were reported by parents of children with visual, hearing, or speech impairments, and the greatest levels of dissatisfaction were reported by parents of students with emotional disturbances.

In addition, satisfaction among parents of children with disabilities varied by ethnicity and income. For example, 48 percent of African American parents, 55 percent of Caucasian parents, and 59 percent of Hispanic parents reported being very satisfied with their children's overall schooling. While income did not affect parents' satisfaction with most aspects of their children's schooling, middle-income and wealthier families were less satisfied with schools' communication efforts. Nineteen percent of families with household incomes of more than $50,000 and 18 percent of those with incomes between $25,000 and $50,000 were dissatisfied with the communication efforts of their children's schools, compared to 12 percent of families with incomes of $25,000 or less.

Last, the survey found that few families who were dissatisfied with their children's schooling entered into formal mediation or due process hearings. Only 11 percent of families of thirteen- to seventeen-year-olds with disabilities reported having been through mediation, and 5 percent reported having been through a due process hearing at some time in their children's school careers. Nonetheless, these survey results underscore the need for schools to develop and implement practices that are inclusive and responsive to the specific needs of families of children with disabilities. (See the summary of a parent interview in Box 4.1.)

Box 4.1   In Pam's Words

Below are excerpts from an interview conducted in December 2007 with Pam, a forty-five-year-old elementary school teacher and mother of three children, one boy and two girls. Her twelve-year-old son, Jon, has a learning disability. During the interview, several themes emerged regarding Jon's disability and her experiences with his teachers and schools. This interview summary is not meant to be representative of all families of children with disabilities but to provide insight into the experiences of one mother and her child.

What has been your personal experience having a child with a disability?

Diagnosing

I began to worry when my son was around two years old, and I noticed that his speech wasn't developing as I thought it should. Around the same time, a family member (my grandmother) noticed that he did not respond to her when she called his name, and she suggested that I get his hearing checked. His pediatrician had never indicated that he had any problems or difficulties, but I asked for a referral, and he provided one to an ear specialist, who then made a referral to a speech therapist and an occupational therapist. At that time, they started considering different diagnoses. They said maybe pervasive developmental disorder or autism because of the lack of eye contact, the humming, and the delayed speech, but they felt it was a mild case and so it was hard to be certain. The therapists would come to the house and work with Jon on his cognitive development with activities like stacking blocks and on his speech development, trying to initiate conversation and get him to talk more. They also connected me to an early preschool program for Jon.

(Continued)

(Continued)

Coping

At first I was in denial, and I thought he would "grow out of it" with the interventions. . . . The therapists were great, and they connected me to services for Jon, but nothing really for me or my husband. All I really wanted to hear back then, though, was that Jon would be okay. . . . I don't think that I came to terms with his disability until maybe when he was in the second or third grade. There was no major event or dramatic experience; I just accepted it.

Networking

I went to a few support group meetings for families with children with autism and even enrolled Jon in a summer camp for children with autism, but I found that Jon functioned at a much higher level than other children in the camp. The stories and experiences that were shared at the support group meetings were so different from what I was experiencing with my son. When I'd speak and share some of my concerns, people would look at me like, "Why are you here? Do you know how lucky you are?" So the autism label doesn't quite fit my son, and I haven't had an opportunity to meet families whose children have learning differences similar to Jon's and who have experiences similar to mine.

Labeling

Jon is labeled learning disabled. There have been questions about what Jon's label should be. My son's current school wants him labeled as autistic as opposed to learning disabled (the district doesn't recognize the label pervasive developmental disorder), although he would not be provided any additional services with a label change. My main issue is that I think it is the responsibility of educators to look for ways to educate children regardless of the label. I sometimes think that some schools are interested in labels to excuse themselves from educating children.

Advocating

I have had good IEP meetings and difficult ones. Of late, they have been difficult, and I have had to request changes in my son's IEP. Really, what kind of parent would I be if I knew that my son should have reading comprehension goals in his IEP and I didn't advocate for them? So when I asked that reading comprehension goals be included in his IEP, the teacher included all these reading comprehension goals but not what my son needed—like identifying the main idea or retelling and sequencing the story—so I requested another meeting. I need to know that the IEP team is taking his needs seriously, and they seem to resent that.

What do you want administrators to do?

Listening

Parents with children with special needs have gone through a lot already as far as having a child identified as learning disabled or learning different and the whole process of accepting that their child has a disability. I mean, that is very difficult. So when their child moves into an educational setting, parents are already fearful about how their child is going to be treated. So I think that administrators should be sensitive to that and know that when parents request services or ask questions or things of that nature they are not trying to be a thorn in their side. They should listen to them with a certain kind of empathy and respect.

Partnering

I think that the needs of families with children with disabilities are slightly different from the needs of other parents. There are things that schools can do to better support families, like they can set up special meetings when children are about to transition to another school. [The district's organization—K–4, 5–6, 7–8, 9, 10–12—results in many transitions for families and students.] Parents can meet the new teachers, administrators, and staff, get familiar with new surroundings, and learn about the services provided. It would also give families with children with disabilities the opportunity to meet each other. . . . Principals should just strive to work with the parents in partnership. They shouldn't approach parents with an attitude like, "This is the school, and this is what we do, and you just 'get in where you fit in.'" You know, that arrogant attitude like, "This is what we do, and you just accept it and be grateful." I told them at my son's last ARD that I think they want parents to be ashamed of their children and come in and just be grateful that they have allowed us [families with children with disabilities] to be in their presence. They behave as if parents should say, "Thank you for allowing my son to come to your school, and whatever you do for him, I'll just be grateful." Sometimes I feel like that is what they want, and I refuse to adopt that attitude.

ENGAGEMENT STRATEGIES FOR FAMILIES OF CHILDREN WITH DISABILITIES

In 1998, two schools that served students with a wide spectrum of disabilities were studied using a qualitative case study approach that included extensive interviews and observations (see Sanders, 2000). The case schools were very successful in involving families and communities in the education of the students using a partnership team approach and Epstein's framework of six types of involvement. Data analysis revealed three processes that allowed these schools to develop comprehensive and inclusive partnerships with their students' families. These processes were (1) creating avenues for communication, (2) opening doors for decision making, and (3) promoting pathways for student progress. Here, we expand on these processes, as well as the importance of schools creating inclusive environments that support families of students with disabilities.

Creating Avenues for Communication

In their text *Special Education for Today's Teachers*, Rosenberg, Westling, and McLeskey (2008) observed:

> Connecting successfully with parents requires a host of interpersonal communication skills such as effective listening, nonjudgmental questioning, flexibility, and compromise. Through open, honest, and positive discussions designed to promote home-school coordination, professional teachers dispel the often-held perception that only appreciative, flattering, uncritical, and non-interfering interactions are welcome at school.

As described in Chapter 2, several studies have emphasized the importance of regular and meaningful communication for effective partnerships. Indeed, communication was central to the partnership program at each of the two case schools studied. Newsletter articles related to ARD and IEP meetings, student transitions, and home activities to support students' learning and progress were written with the input of each school's social worker, principal, general and special education teachers, and parent leaders. As members of the schools' partnership teams, they met regularly to discuss how to provide parents of children with disabilities with relevant timely information to help them understand special education within the context of the school and to keep them informed about special events and meeting dates related to their children's learning.

Of importance, the communication strategies employed by the case schools shared three common features: communications were informative, caring, and creative.

Informative

School communications were informative; in other words, they included relevant, accurate, and timely material of interest and importance to their students' families. Communications covered topics such as the ARD process, inclusion, student transitions, home activities to support students' learning and progress, and other topics that helped build families' capacity to support their children's learning and development. While being informative, these communications avoided the "formalism" that can hinder home-school partnerships. According to Howland, Anderson, Smiley, and Abbott (2006), "'Formalism' in typical communication between parents and special education professionals . . . has perpetuated the overuse of technical language, hierarchical relationships, and one-way communication, all of which serve to relegate parents to the role of recipient of professional judgment versus empowered participants in their child's education" (p. 49). By avoiding formalism, the schools provided families with important information that established a foundation for two-way communication and home-school collaboration.

Caring

Home-school communications at the case schools were also caring. When discussing the importance of caring in schools, Lipsitz (1995) argued that "without caring individual human beings cannot thrive." Noddings (1995) contended, "Our society does not need to make its children first in mathematics and science. It needs to care for its children." Chaskin and Rauner (1995) stated, "It is the continual expression of caring behaviors that develops the trusting relationships in which growth can occur." Caring school communities, then, are sensitive to the needs and concerns of their students and families and express this sensitivity through their words and actions. Whether verbally during school meetings and visits, or in writing through memos and newsletters, home-school communications at the case schools reflected understanding and respect for families and students.

Creative

Finally, schools employed creative means to disseminate information. The case schools used games at PTO meetings to help families decipher the acronyms involved in the special education process (see Box 4.2 for common acronyms in special education) and had bus aides hand out flyers to families at the bus stop. The schools also used telephone calling systems to remind families of events or to summarize events families could not attend. One case school developed special logs on which teachers could systematically document the date, time, and purpose of their calls to families. Communications that were informative, caring, and creative helped the case schools and families build the mutual support central to successful programs of school, family, and community partnerships.

Box 4.2   Common Acronyms in Special Education*

ARD—Admission, Review, and Dismissal. Another name for the local education agency committee that determines whether a student is in need of special education services and, if so, what services.

(Continued)

(Continued)

IDEA—Individuals with Disabilities Education Act. The federal law that provides the legal authority for early intervention and special educational services for children from birth to age twenty-one. Part B outlines services for children ages three to twenty-one. Part C outlines services for children from birth to age three.

IEP—Individualized Education Program. A written statement of a child's current level of educational performance and an individualized plan of instruction, including the goals, specific services to be received, the staff who will carry out the services, the standards and timelines for evaluating progress, and the amount and degree to which the child will participate with typically developing peers.

LRE—Least Restrictive Environment. The placement that is as close as possible to the general education environment. This educational setting is the one that permits a child to receive the most educational benefit while still participating in a regular educational environment to the maximum extent appropriate. LRE is a requirement under IDEA.

*For a more extensive list of acronyms in special education, see www .tourettesyndrome.net

Opening Doors for Decision Making

The case schools also encouraged parents' involvement in school decisions that affected their children and the larger school environment. The schools did so by soliciting parents' ideas and opinions and demystifying structures and processes in special education. For example, at a special meeting, school and parent leaders used creative activities such as games and skits to promote understanding of special education processes and procedures. The school did so because it found that many families were confused by the special education process and were therefore less likely to become involved in decision-making opportunities. A parent member of one school's partnership team explained, "There was ARD, IEP, MOIL, SPH—all these initials. I know when I came in, I did not know what these things were. I was too intimidated to ask, and I felt stupid. I felt that they knew what they were talking about. . . . I did not say one word."

The special parent meeting was designed so that parents would have the opportunity to meet and interact with school personnel and faculty working with their children, asking questions and sharing concerns with others in a nonstressful, nonjudgmental environment. The meeting was also a vehicle for the school to encourage families to become active, not passive, participants in the decision-making process. For example, the principal used the meeting as an opportunity to stress the importance of parents' participation in ARD meetings:

> My comment [to the parents] was, "This is more important than your child's birthday. This is more important than Christmas because we are going to decide the educational program for your child. If we make a decision that you don't agree with, you can appeal through due process." We tell them the person who handles appeals. We give them the person's name and telephone number, . . . so our parents leave here understanding, I hope, what their rights are, what the process is, and that they don't have to accept anything that they don't think is best for their child.

The meeting helped the school increase its family attendance at ARD meetings by 15 percent in one year.

Equally important is family participation in IEP meetings. In 2004, revisions were made to IDEA that require parent participation in the development of an IEP. More specifically, the IEP team should be composed of the following:

- The parents of a child with a disability
- Not less than one regular education teacher of the child
- Not less than one special education teacher (or where appropriate, provider) of the child
- A representative of the local education agency (LEA) who is qualified to provide or supervise the provision of specially designed instruction to meet the unique needs of children with disabilities, knowledgeable about the general education curriculum, and knowledgeable about the available resources of the LEA
- An individual who can interpret the instructional implications of evaluation results, who may be a member of the team described above
- At the discretion of the parents or the agency, other individuals who have knowledge or expertise regarding the child, including related services personnel as appropriate and, whenever appropriate, the child with a disability [614(d)(1)(B)]

While the 2004 revisions to IDEA establish when IEP team meeting attendance is not necessary [614(d)(1)(C)(i), (iii)] and when IEP team members might be excused from attending an IEP meeting [614(d)(1)(C)(ii), (iii)], the expectation is that families and school and district personnel will work collaboratively to develop the IEP, the controlling document of services for children with disabilities.

Several studies have highlighted the important role schools play in creating environments conducive to parent involvement in the IEP process

(Harry, Allen, & McLaughlin, 1995; Miles-Bonart, 2002; Munn-Joseph & Gavin-Evans, 2008; Salas, 2004). Recognizing schools' importance, Turnbull and Turnbull (in Turnbull et al., 1995, p. 77) identified several strategies for increasing parent involvement in IEP meetings. In summary, the authors suggested that before the meeting the schools should

1. solicit information from the family about their preferences and needs regarding the conference;

2. arrange a convenient time and location for the meeting; and

3. assist families with logistical issues such as transportation and childcare.

During the meeting, the school administrator and school/district personnel should

1. greet students, families, and their advocates;

2. ask if family members desire clarification of their legal rights;

3. avoid educational jargon as much as possible and clarify diagnostic terminology throughout the meeting; and

4. collaboratively generate appropriate goals and objectives for all subject areas requiring special instruction consistent with expectations.

After the meeting, the school administrator or designated personnel should

1. summarize orally and on paper the major decisions and follow-up responsibilities of all participants; and

2. express appreciation to all participants for their help in the decision-making process.

These strategies help promote the type of communication and exchange that studies have linked to productive and satisfying IEP meetings. Without school efforts to promote this type of communication, many families feel pushed out of the decision-making process. Salas (2004) interviewed ten Mexican American mothers over one school year to better understand how they felt about their experiences during IEP meetings. She found that, although the mothers wanted to be involved in decisions regarding their children's educational plans, they were silenced by overt and covert messages that their input was not valued. Miles-Bonart (2002), however, found that a strong relationship exists between clear and respectful communication among IEP team members and parental satisfaction.

Miles-Bonart (2002) also found a strong relationship between the presence of proper personnel at IEP meetings and parental satisfaction. Thus, a key role schools can play in promoting greater parent involvement in IEP meetings is to schedule these meetings so that parents and all necessary members of the IEP team are present and that sufficient time is allotted for discussion, questions, and consensus building. School principals, as building leaders and professional role models, play a critical role in creating schools that encourage and support greater family involvement in IEP meetings (see Box 4.3).

Box 4.3   The Role of Administrators in Increasing Parent Involvement in IEP Meetings

Administrators should

- organize training for professionals and parents on stages of the IEP process from identification of the disability to implementation and evaluation of IEP services;
- actively and competently engage in IEP meetings and serve as role models in the IEP process;
- ensure class coverage for teachers to ensure participation in IEP meetings; and
- work with others in the school building to create a comfortable, collaborative climate for IEP meetings.

Source: Miles-Bonart, S. (2002). A look at variables affecting parent satisfaction with IEP meetings. In *No Child Left Behind: The vital role of rural schools.* 22nd Annual National Conference Proceedings of the American Council on Rural Special Education, March 7–9, 2002, Reno, Nevada.

Promoting Pathways for Student Progress

The third process that emerged as central to the case schools' success in developing comprehensive partnership programs was their focus on student progress. According to Epstein (1986), the form of involvement families are most interested in is how they can help their children with learning at home. Indeed, research in the United States and abroad has shown that, when families get involved with students' learning at home, students' attitudes toward learning and school performance improve. Although some families are involved with their children's learning and progress at home without assistance, most parents report that they could better help if the teachers guided them in what to do at home and helped them become more knowledgeable about their children's needs (SEARCH Institute, 2002). This was a primary goal at both schools in the study.

Essentially, the two processes previously described—two-way communication and parental involvement in decision making—were integrally linked to students' intellectual and socioemotional growth and development. Through newsletters, surveys, notebooks, home and school visits, and telephone calls, educators and parents shared information and made decisions about students' progress and what to do to promote that progress. At each school, parent, school, and community resources were mobilized to encourage multiple pathways for students' progress.

For example, at one school's final PTO meeting for the school year, families and school staff gathered for a meal; then each teacher went to a preassigned classroom. Parents first went to their children's classroom teacher, and the teacher described and demonstrated an activity that parents could perform with their children during the summer. The demonstration lasted fifteen minutes, and parents were given the materials they would need to carry out the activity. Parents then attended a maximum of three other demonstrations conducted by classroom teachers, the home arts teacher, the speech therapist, and others to gather additional ideas on activities to conduct with their child during the summer months.

Although this was a culminating activity for the school, families and communities were given opportunities throughout the year to help promote students' learning. The school had volunteers from a local university who tutored and mentored selected students under the supervision of the classroom teacher. They interacted with students on a number of classroom activities and art projects and were showcased on the school's central bulletin board.

The school's nurse also led parent workshops on issues such as toileting for the families of severely disabled students. These workshops were designed to provide parents with information and activities they could use at home to help students master these skills. The school also had an open door policy. Families were encouraged to come in and see what their children were working on at school so they could follow up at home. Classroom teachers sent home a checklist of the tasks that students with IEPs performed at school and asked families to indicate if children were performing these tasks at home. When there were discrepancies, teachers and parents discussed what could be done so that student progress was better supported in both environments.

One teacher on the school's partnership team had a student whose parent reported that the child could not do any of the tasks he was able to successfully perform at school. According to the teacher,

> I asked her to come in, and she not only came, she brought the [child's] aunt and the stepfather. I encouraged her to stay in the background. He [the student] did not know that she was anywhere in the building. . . . She observed him not only performing the self-help skills, she also observed him playing and interacting with other children; she observed him choosing a toy. And when she came in,

she apologized. And now I know that she is doing more at home because I see a change in his behavior. She said, "I never knew that he could do this." Some of our parents need that encouragement.

Another family member on the school's partnership team added, "You have to have a connection with the teachers, parents, schools, and the community so that the child can be embraced fully. That's the only way to achieve progress." As part of No Child Left Behind, schools are currently being held responsible for the "adequate yearly progress" of all students, including those with disabilities. A partnership approach should be a part of each school's efforts to achieve this goal.

CREATING INCLUSIVE ENVIRONMENTS FOR FAMILIES OF CHILDREN WITH DISABILITIES

To realize the goals and spirit of IDEA, as well as achieve excellent partnership programs, schools must strive not only to create avenues of communication, to open doors to decision making, and to promote pathways to progress but also to include families of children with disabilities in *all* activities. To do so, schools should make sure that their facilities are not only handicap accessible but handicap friendly. For example, during school events that draw large crowds, schools can have alternative entrances and exits for individuals who require more time or space (e.g., those using wheelchairs and other mobility aids) to enter and leave the buildings. Schools should also consider how rooms are arranged and whether there is sufficient space and appropriate seating for individuals with physical disabilities. Finally, schools should determine the need and, as appropriate, arrange for sign interpreters to ensure that all members of the school community have access to information being shared at school meetings and events and should use large fonts in written correspondence and school presentations. Attending to such small but critical details can make the difference in whether families with disabilities feel welcomed or excluded.

Schools should also strive to meet the special needs of families of children with disabilities during events such as Back to School nights, parent-teacher and parent-teacher-student conferences, and Family Fun and Learning nights. Back to School nights should include opportunities for families to meet all grade-level teachers and staff, including special educators and assistants. The entire school community should know the resources available to students with special needs and their families. Schools should also consider having a special session either before or after the general Back to School night to address the questions of families of students with IEPs that the general presentations by grade-level teachers may not address. Extended time would also provide families of children with disabilities the opportunity to meet one another.

Families of children with disabilities desire information about their children's specific disabilities and the best resources and services available to them. The families of older children also desire information on how to support the transition of their children from secondary school to appropriate postsecondary educational institutions, employment training, or respite care. McDermott (2008) contends that this type of information can be provided in parent groups where families have opportunities to share experiences, expertise, and insights. These types of support groups or networks can be face to face; alternatively, experienced and novice parents or parents whose children share similar disabilities can be paired and their interaction telephone or email based. By supporting the development of parent networks, schools increase families' access to support and information that can help them better understand and advocate for their children's special education needs (Munn-Joseph & Gavin-Evans, 2008; Sheldon, 2002).

Schools can also provide parents with information about national networks that provide resources, support, and training to families who have members with disabilities (see Box 4.4). Although school-based and national parent networks can be important sources of information for many families, schools cannot simply relinquish this responsibility to parent networks. As previously described, schools must also develop two-way systems to share information with parents of special education students. Parents need to be able to express their concerns and need for resources, and school personnel need to be prepared to respond and support those parents.

Box 4.4   National Support Networks for Families of Children With Disabilities*

Support for Families of Children With Disabilities, http://www.supportfor families.org/internetguide: This site organizes a variety of Internet resources for the families of children with disabilities. The site is divided into nine categories: (1) getting started, (2) the laws, (3) parent sites, (4) specific disabilities, (5) education, (6) health, (7) mental health, (8) transition to adulthood, and (9) Español.

The Father's Network, http://www.fathersnetwork.org/: This site provides up-to-date information and resources for fathers, family members, and care providers of children with disabilities and chronic illnesses.

National Native American Families Together, http://www.nipic.org/: This site provides information (printed, by email, phone, and workshops) on disability issues for Native family members who have children with disabilities and the professionals who work with them.

National Association for the Education of African American Children with Learning Disabilities, http://www.aacld.org/: This site provides information to increase awareness and understanding of the specific issues facing African American children with disabilities. It seeks to link information and resources provided by an established network of individuals and organizations experienced in minority research and special education with parents, educators, and others responsible for providing a quality education for all students.

---

*This information is provided as an example of resources available to families of students with disabilities and not as an endorsement of any specific organization.

Furthermore, schools should consider extending the time allotted for parent-teacher and parent-teacher-student conferences for the families of children with disabilities. Because these meetings may include others working directly with the child and involve extended conversations focused on specific objectives in IEPs, more time may be needed than is usually allotted. Finally, many schools have Family Fun and Learning nights to provide families with strategies they can use at home to support their children's learning in mathematics, science, reading, and other topics. Grade-level teachers and special educators should work collaboratively to ensure that such events also include sessions that provide appropriate strategies and supports for students with disabilities. In these ways, schools can ensure that the needs of all children and families are met and send a clear message of inclusion and collaboration to the families of children with disabilities.

WHY THIS MATTERS FOR PRINCIPALS

Many schools are working to improve home-school partnerships, yet some families may not be reached sufficiently through the efforts employed. One such population is the families of students with disabilities. While IDEA and its reauthorizations have specified parental rights in the education of children with disabilities, there are no "written rights" for the full inclusion of families of these children in schools' partnership efforts. As IDEA currently exists, school-family relationships are based on procedure, not partnership.

As school leaders, principals establish the tone at a school and are highly influential actors who shape how school staff and practitioners treat families with special education children. Principals can work with faculty, staff, community members, and families to ensure that school meetings and events are responsive to the needs of families of children with disabilities. Principals can also play a critical role in supporting families' involvement in IEP meetings and other decision-making opportunities. When principals do so, they help ensure that schools' partnership efforts meet legislative requirements and, more important, promote the success of all students, including those with special needs.

Action Steps for School Leaders

✓ Work with faculty and staff to create a school environment that respects differences, including learning differences.

✓ Work with the partnership team to arrange annual opportunities for families with children with disabilities to meet with faculty and staff to share information, questions, and concerns.

✓ Work with families, feeder schools, and other feeder institutions to facilitate the smooth transition of students with disabilities.

✓ Ensure that the partnership team includes at least one special educator and/or parent of a child with disabilities.

REFLECTION QUESTIONS

1. Do you believe that families of students with disabilities have unique partnership needs that schools should address? Explain.

2. How have the families of students with disabilities been rendered visible or invisible at your school? What do you believe are the factors that have influenced your school's actions toward the families of students with disabilities?

3. How does your school approach and schedule IEP meetings for special needs students? How are parents encouraged to participate beyond providing a required signature? How have parents responded? What factors might account for their responses?

5

Linguistically Diverse Families and School, Family, and Community Partnerships

This chapter discusses growing diversity in the United States and the concomitant increase in the numbers of Limited English Proficient (LEP) families. It describes NCLB requirements for school outreach to LEP families and strategies that can support this outreach. Finally, it discusses the importance of principal leadership for the success of such efforts.

GROWTH IN IMMIGRATION AND LIMITED ENGLISH PROFICIENT (LEP) STUDENTS AND FAMILIES

Over the last decade, U.S. public school students have become more linguistically diverse, with a growing population of students identified as Limited English Proficient (LEP) or English Language Learners (ELL).[1] This diversity has been accelerated by historically high rates of immigration to the United States. During the 1990s, between 14 and 16 million immigrants entered the country, up from 10 million in the 1980s and 7 million in the 1970s. In 2000, children of immigrant parents represented one in five (20 percent) of all children under the age of eighteen. About 75 percent of these children were born in the United States, while approximately one-quarter were foreign-born (Capps et al., 2005).

There is great diversity in origin among immigrants to the United States, but the largest portion come from Mexico. In 2000, 38 percent of foreign-born students were born in Mexico. In addition to Mexico, the most frequent countries of origin for immigrant children in grades preK–5 were India (3.4 percent), Canada (3.3 percent), the Philippines (3.1 percent), and China (3.1 percent). For older students (grades 6–12), the most frequent countries of origin for immigrant children were the Philippines (3.5 percent), the Dominican Republic (3.4 percent), Vietnam (3.3 percent), and El Salvador (3.3 percent). Other countries of origin such as Korea, Russia, and Haiti each produce less than 3 percent of foreign-born children in U.S. public schools. Furthermore, countries of origin for immigrant populations differ by state so that some states may have more Russian families and children, while others have more Korean families and children (Capps et al., 2005).

Students with immigrant parents are concentrated in six states: California, Texas, New York, Florida, Illinois, and New Jersey. However, these states are not the states with the fastest-growing number of children of immigrant parents. Between 1990 and 2000, Nevada, North Carolina, Georgia, Nebraska, Arkansas, Arizona, and South Dakota experienced over 100 percent growth in the number of public school students in grades preK–5 from immigrant families. The average rate of growth in the number of children of immigrant parents in the United States from 1990 to 2000 was 39 percent (Capps et al., 2005). These immigration trends suggest that states throughout the country will continue to experience growing numbers of LEP students and families in their public schools (National Association for the Education of Young Children [NAEYC], 2008). Consequently, many schools that historically have had culturally and linguistically homogeneous populations must now develop strategies to communicate with students and families who are not native English speakers.

LEP STUDENTS AND FAMILIES

Although immigration has helped fuel the growing LEP population in U.S. schools, most children of immigrants are not LEP. In 2000, 10.8 million school-age children were children of immigrants, but only about 3.4 million were LEP. The majority of these LEP students were U.S.-born children

---

[1] In this chapter, LEP and ELL are used to describe children and families who do not speak, read, and write English well. Definitions of LEP and ELL populations, however, may differ by state and school district.

of immigrant parents or U.S.-born children of U.S.-born parents who live in linguistically isolated households and communities where little English is spoken. For example, in 2000, 59 percent of LEP students in grades K–5 and 27 percent of LEP students in grades 6–12 were U.S.-born children of immigrants. Eighteen percent of LEP students in grades K–5 and 29 percent of LEP students in grades 6–12 were U.S.-born children of U.S.-born parents. Only 24 percent of LEP children in grades preK–5 and 44 percent of LEP children in grades 6–12 were foreign-born (Capps et al., 2005).

About three-quarters of all LEP students in grades preK–5 and 72 percent of students in grades 6–12 speak a dialect of Spanish. Other less frequently spoken languages include Chinese, Vietnamese, Korean, Hmong/Miao, French/Haitian Creole, Russian, Arabic, and Tagalog (Capps et al., 2005). This diversity, along with the diversity of dialects within each broad language category, can present major challenges to schools and other institutions responsible for providing services to immigrant children and families.

Moreover, most LEP students and their families are low income, qualifying for the free and reduced-price meals programs. In 2000, 68 percent of LEP children in grades preK–5 and 60 percent of LEP students in grades 6–12 were low income. These rates were almost twice the rate of their English proficient counterparts. Consequently, schools seeking to create stronger connections with LEP families must often address challenges associated with creating partnerships with low-income families as well. (See Chapter 6 for more on this topic.)

Parents of LEP students are also generally less educated than the parents of English proficient students. In 2000, 48 percent of LEP children compared to 11 percent of English proficient students in grades preK–5 had parents with less than a high school diploma. Twenty-five percent of LEP children compared to 2 percent of English proficient students in grades preK–5 had parents with less than a ninth-grade education. In grades 6–12, 35 percent of LEP children compared to 9 percent of English proficient students had parents with less than a high school diploma or GED, and 26 percent compared to 4 percent had parents with less than a ninth-grade education (Capps et al., 2005). Schools, then, must also consider the literacy levels of their LEP families when developing outreach strategies.

LEP STUDENTS AND NCLB

Currently, the No Child Left Behind (NCLB) Act of 2002 holds schools accountable for the academic performance and progress of LEP students and for reaching out to LEP students' families. Title I of NCLB requires that schools improve the performance of LEP students on reading and mathematics assessments beginning in third grade. A central purpose of Title III of NCLB is to "ensure that LEP children, including immigrant children and youth, attain English proficiency, develop a high level of academic attainment in English, and meet the same standards expected of all children" (U.S. Department of Education, 2005).

NCLB also extends certain rights to the families of LEP students. The legislation requires schools to inform all parents of their children's progress on assessments and their options and rights if the school fails to make AYP over time. In addition to these general requirements that apply to all families, NCLB requires schools to inform the parents of LEP children about the type of language instruction their children are receiving and of their right to refuse bilingual or ESL instruction for their children. NCLB also requires schools to communicate with parents in the language they speak to the extent "practicable" (U.S. Department of Education, 2004).

To achieve these mandates and educate all students to realize their full potential, schools must find ways to effectively partner with LEP students' families. Schools seeking to partner with the parents of LEP students must be prepared to address issues related to language, culture, literacy, poverty, and, for undocumented immigrant families, fear of detection and deportation, in addition to students' academic programs and progress. The following section describes four strategies: creating a welcoming school environment, promoting cultural awareness among educators, providing learning opportunities for LEP families, and engaging in culturally responsive communication practices that schools can implement to achieve these objectives. The final section in this chapter discusses the principal's role in supporting these strategies.

STRATEGIES TO FACILITATE THE INVOLVEMENT OF LEP FAMILIES

Creating a Welcoming School Environment

Henderson, Mapp, Johnson, and Davies (2007) suggest that to create schools where *all* students and families feel welcome, school leaders should attempt to see their schools, both the exterior and interior, through the eyes of a stranger to assess its accessibility and appeal. Questions that can guide such assessments include (1) Are the school grounds well maintained? (2) Is the school entrance clearly identifiable? (3) Are there individuals or signs to guide visitors to the front office? (4) Are these signs in the native languages of LEP students enrolled in the school? (5) Is the school clean and well maintained? (6) Is student work posted throughout the building? (7) Are student and visitor restrooms clean? and (8) Is there a parent room or area where families can gather with one another, faculty, and staff to share information, complete volunteer assignments, or plan events? Making the necessary adjustments to ensure the building is welcoming is the first step for many schools in strengthening family and community engagement.

Once the physical structure of the school is made welcoming, schools need to ensure that all families feel that their presence, cultures, and contributions are needed and valued. This task is directly related to building the trusting relationships essential to effective school, family, and community partnerships discussed in Chapter 2. To achieve this objective, many culturally and linguistically diverse schools implement activities that showcase the school's diversity and help families, students, faculty, and staff learn about and celebrate one another's cultures. These activities, such as International Night at Prairie Elementary School in Naperville, Illinois, can include community partners, be co-planned with community-based organizations, or be open to the larger community to emphasize the school's connection to the community as a whole (Box 5.1). Such annual events held at the beginning of the academic year can send a clear message that the school values all its students and families and the diversity they represent. These events can also reduce the isolation often felt by LEP students and their families.

Box 5.1   International Night "Around the World in 90 Minutes"

Prairie Elementary School, Naperville, Illinois

Some of the international families with children at Prairie Elementary were feeling isolated from others at the school. They talked with the teacher of English Language Learners (ELL) about wanting to be more involved with the school and with their children's education. So the school decided to conduct an International Night to welcome these families and help them connect with others at this celebration of cultures.

Building on last year's successful international "Games Around the World," the Action Team for Partnerships (ATP) decided to expand the event this year to include food, music, art, and dance. With the theme, "Around the World in 90 Minutes" and a hot air balloon to carry the idea, International Night took off, with adventures galore.

Each family was invited to share its heritage with a display of interesting facts, photos, and artifacts, and to bring a food or prepared dish from its cuisine. Students, teachers, and parents traveled around the school to

- view cultural displays that highlighted fun facts about many families' native countries;
- sample ethnic foods prepared by families;
- get creative with international crafts, including Chinese character writing, origami, and German paper cutting;
- learn traditional Hebrew songs or participate in an African stone-passing game; and
- learn to salsa dance.

The ATP designed a passport that included each activity and its country of origin. The passports included interesting facts about each country and space for a stamp on each page as families visited the various activities.

(Continued)

(Continued)

Throughout the evening, the organizers gave away international board games as raffle prizes. Winners were announced every 10 to 15 minutes throughout the evening. During each announcement, families were reminded to explore the various activities.

Members of the ATP oversaw the entire event, which required considerable planning and coordination. Many team members volunteered to teach games, crafts, or music. Other volunteers coordinated the food tables. Community partners contributed, too. A local dance instructor taught salsa to families, and a neighborhood business donated the Italian ice cream, Gelato, for sampling.

One of the challenges was communicating with some of the ELL families who do not speak English. To overcome this, the ATP met with the families about six weeks before the event and stayed in close contact with the ELL instructor, who communicated instructions to the families, making sure everyone understood what they needed to do.

In addition to encouraging parent involvement, the International Night enriched children's knowledge of social studies and enhanced their cultural awareness. All Prairie families were able to appreciate and enjoy the cultural diversity within the school. As a result, ELL families seem to feel more welcome. The event was well attended, with 140 students and 80 parents present. When the ATP solicited informal feedback from attendees and volunteers, many commented on how much fun the evening was. The ELL instructor said she had never seen her students look so happy and confident.

Barbara Ryan, School/Family/Community Partnership Co-chair

Source: Maushard, M., Martin, C., Hutchins, D., Greenfeld, M., Thomas, B., Fournier, A., & Pickett, G. (Eds.). (2007). *Promising partnership practices 2007.* Baltimore, MD: National Network of Partnership Schools. Reprinted with permission, © 2007 National Network of Partnership Schools, Johns Hopkins University.

Promoting Cultural Awareness

As described previously, LEP students and families are ethnically, linguistically, economically, and experientially diverse. Because of this diversity, a key strategy to engage greater numbers of LEP parents in their students' education is to learn as much as possible about the language, culture, lifestyles, educational expectations, and concerns of the specific LEP population(s) enrolled in the school. When faculty and staff are prepared to understand the beliefs and values of diverse cultural groups and how these beliefs and values may conflict or correspond with the values and beliefs of the school, as well as structural barriers that may limit parent involvement among diverse groups, they are better able to account for these differences in their classroom and family outreach practices (Weiss, Kreider, Lopez, & Chatman, 2005).

For example, Fu (2004), when discussing the perceptions of family involvement among Chinese immigrants, observed:

> For most of the new Chinese immigrants in Chinatown, there is no time for volunteering at school, and they feel inadequate assisting their children with their schoolwork. If we see their absence at school as disinterest, then how can we explain the fact that they bring their children to this country for what they deem a superior education? Chinatown residents have told me recently that fathers bring their children to this country and leave their wives in China because it is very hard to get visas for the entire family. In order not to delay their children's education in the U.S., many couples prefer to be separated physically themselves rather than to leave their children in China. This separation could last 10 years or even longer. Obviously, their children's educational welfare is the impetus behind their emigration. For this goal, they are willing to sacrifice nearly everything. (p. 21)

In Chapter 2, we discussed the importance of a multidimensional approach to family involvement that acknowledges and supports home-based, school-based, and home-school communication involvement practices. When this multidimensional approach is implemented with knowledge of and respect for cultural diversity, educators can create inclusive classrooms and schools where all families are helped to contribute to their children's school success in ways that reflect and complement family and community strengths. Schools can also help LEP families expand, modify, or refine their current practices to better align with the school's goals for students' learning, or to better address the needs of their individual child (DiCerbo, 2000). See Box 5.2, Celebrate Our Differences.

Box 5.2   Celebrate Our Differences

El Rancho Elementary School, Chino, California

A bilingual presentation complete with translation headphones was the key to bringing together the school community at El Rancho Elementary School this past winter. On February 28, 2008, the school's Action Team for Partnerships (ATP) hosted the Celebrate Our Differences workshop for parents and teachers to encourage more open lines of communication between the two groups.

Administrators at El Rancho face many challenges in helping all students succeed in school. Among its students, 41 percent are non-English speakers and 85 percent participate in the free and reduced-price lunch program.

(Continued)

(Continued)

Cultural misconceptions and stereotypes among teachers, students, and families were growing. The ATP decided to reduce tensions and build cultural bridges by hosting Celebrate Our Differences. They began by advertising the multicultural event in the school newsletter, on the school Web site, through fliers, and in the local newspaper.

Preparing for the workshop was truly a group effort! Hispanic parents decorated the school's multipurpose room, and the PTA hospitality committee organized refreshments. School administrators encouraged all teachers to attend the event by providing a stipend. About fifty students and seventy-five parents participated in the workshop. After a few icebreaker games, administrators divided the attendees into small groups. Each group received a giant, poster-sized sticky note pad and some writing instruments. They were given a series of questions about their children's education and asked to post their ideas in both Spanish and English.

For the next hour, the small groups of parents, teachers, and students discussed questions such as, "What are ways parents can show their children that they care about their education?" and "How can we build a communication bridge without barriers?" At the end of the discussion, each group presented their findings to the full group. At the end of the evening, a school staff member gave a moving speech, summarizing the general findings of the assembly for all.

In perhaps the most dramatic twist of the evening, the general presentation was conducted entirely in Spanish, while English-speaking attendees listened to their peers talk through a translator on special headsets. For many folks, this was the most interesting element of the night. Disoriented by the double speaking, some chose to turn off their headphones for a bit and understand what they could in Spanish. Others found it interesting to hear their own English phrases translated back through their headsets. "It was very, very powerful for me, personally, to walk in someone else's shoes," a program specialist commented after the workshop.

Spanish-speaking parents were pleased to have their language spotlighted. "I want to thank you for presenting this evening's event in Spanish and making us feel welcome," a Spanish-speaking mother wrote. Since the activity, teachers have noticed a dramatic increase in the number of parents at parent-teacher conferences, setting record attendance levels at the school. The school plans to repeat the event on an annual basis. They hope that even more parents will take an active leadership role in next year's workshop.

Kelly Erin Blacher, Librarian/Parent Coordinator

Source: Hutchins, D., Maushard, M., O'Donnell, C., Greenfeld, M., & Thomas, B. (Eds.). (2008). *Promising partnership practices 2008.* Baltimore, MD: National Network of Partnership Schools. Reprinted with permission, © 2008 National Network of Partnership Schools, Johns Hopkins University.

Providing Learning Opportunities

In addition to building LEP parents' capacity to support their children's learning and school success, schools can help family members increase their own human capital and belief in their ability to help their children learn. For example, Doris Dickson Elementary School in Chino, California, implemented a partnership activity to achieve two goals: (1) to improve parents' English and computer skills and (2) to increase parents' advocacy for their children (see Box 5.3). However, schools do not have to conduct such efforts alone. Many communities have literacy initiatives. By being aware of such opportunities and acting as resource brokers (see Chapter 2), schools can help families gain the skills and sense of efficacy that have been linked to increased parent involvement (Hoover-Dempsey, Walker, & Sandler, 2005).

Box 5.3   Dickson Learning Community

Doris Dickson Elementary School, Chino, California

English and computer classes for parents helped administrators at Doris Dickson Elementary bridge the gap between home and school and overcome some of the school's language challenges. The Dickson Learning Community classes helped twenty-five Spanish-speaking mothers learn English and pick up some computer skills, both of which helped them advocate more successfully for their children.

Nearly 22 percent of students at the school are English Language Learners, and a sizable number of parents speak little or no English. Despite these conditions, Dickson set a school improvement goal to increase all students' English language skills by one grade level each year.

The English classes for parents tied into this goal. They grew out of another parent involvement program at Dickson—the Family Stories class. When that program ended, parents told the Title I resource teacher that they wanted to spend more time together to learn English and to practice their computer skills.

The teacher found a time and a place for the new classes. Originally, it was not clear that the school had enough computers for the parents, but after corralling a few retired laptops, she was able to accommodate the parents. She asked the students who had attended Family Stories to advertise the new classes to other interested parents. Administrators promoted the class in a bilingual flier sent home with students. They also announced the program at a well-attended open house.

Between fifteen and twenty-five parents attended the Friday morning sessions to work on their English and technology skills. Each session began with a forty-five-minute lesson on English grammar or vocabulary, followed by thirty minutes to practice speaking English (no Spanish allowed). Classes usually

(Continued)

(Continued)

ended with a short computer demonstration, teaching mothers about important educational Web sites or how to use email. Volunteers provided childcare for each session so that the parents could focus on their work.

By the end of the school year, teachers and parents had become thoroughly enmeshed in the learning experience. Many parents were so enthusiastic that they asked for weekly vocabulary tests. The principal noted that the parents in the class seemed to feel more comfortable at the school. The resource teacher donated her time to make the classes happen. She and others plan to continue the classes and hope to attract more parents to the Friday morning group.

Source: Hutchins, D., Maushard, M., O'Donnell, C., Greenfeld, M., & Thomas, B. (Eds.). (2008). *Promising partnership practices 2008.* Baltimore, MD: National Network of Partnership Schools. Reprinted with permission, © 2008 National Network of Partnership Schools, Johns Hopkins University.

Culturally Responsive Communication Practices

A study of twenty parents of LEP students in Texas identified parents' desire to communicate with school personnel about their children's school performance and progress as a primary motivator for becoming involved (Cassity & Harris, 2000). More specifically, the author found that the factor most likely to motivate parental involvement in education was the opportunity to ask about their child's behavior. Additional sources of motivation were parents' desire to demonstrate their commitment to their children's education, to learn course information, to share information about their children with teachers, and to inquire about their children's academic progress. The survey also suggested that the parents became involved to obtain information on how to support learning in the home.

Several studies of diverse populations corroborate the importance of home-school communication for parent involvement and students' educational success (Epstein, 2001; Westat and Policy Studies Associates, 2001). Therefore, schools' efforts to involve the families of ELLs should include strategies to promote two-way communication as described in Chapter 2. It is important that the content of these communications include specific opportunities for educators to learn about parents' goals, expectations, and concerns about their children's schooling and to ensure that families have the information they need to better understand the schools' goals, expectations, and concerns about their children's schooling. Furthermore, it is important that the families of LEP students are given ample and ongoing opportunities to learn about the educational pipeline in the United States and the rights and responsibilities of students and families (Cassity & Harris, 2000).

To ensure that these communication efforts reach LEP families, schools should focus not only on *what* they communicate but also on *how* they communicate. By employing a variety of communication strategies and translating school information, schools can improve home-school communication with LEP families.

Use a Variety of Communication Strategies

Many teachers and schools rely on written forms of home-school communication. However, a reliance on written communication places illiterate, low-literacy, and limited English proficient families at a disadvantage. Teachers, then, should explore additional means of communication to establish relationships and communicate with these families. Home and community visits, for example, have been shown to be extremely effective (Meyer & Mann, 2006). Such visits provide teachers with opportunities to better understand their students' homes and communities as well as to express a sincere concern for students and families. When it is necessary to use written forms of communication, teachers should ensure that the language used is accessible to as broad an audience as possible. This means communicating in the native language when possible and keeping the language clear and free from educational jargon.

Employ Translators

Translators can help teachers communicate more effectively with parents who do not share a common language with the school. Although finding appropriate translators is possible and prevalent in some contexts, in others it is very difficult. In such cases, schools should consider soliciting support from community organizations, such as ethnic and faith-based organizations as well as colleges and universities that may have foreign language departments. Translating materials for educational purposes, however, requires a global understanding of the intent of the message and the content to be conveyed (Colina & Sykes, 2004). Therefore, when considering using individuals outside the school system as translators, schools must provide clear guidelines to help them in this bridging role. Schools must also consider district guidelines and restrictions related to translators and translated materials and the sensitivity of the content to be communicated (e.g., inviting families to a school event versus conveying information about a disciplinary action or decision).

Schools can also investigate professional language translation services through the Internet. A free online translation service, Free Translation (http://www.freetranslation.com), provides text and Web page translation from English to Spanish, French, German, Italian, and Portuguese, as well as from Spanish, French, and German to English. According to Joe

Slowinski (2000), educational technology policy analyst, "Because these translations are created by software packages rather than human translators, absolute accuracy might be an issue. But if they are used to share a general understanding of the material, they can be an effective support system for learning and communication" (p. 1). Other Web-based resources can assist educators in standardizing translations in specific languages. For example, Real Academia Española (http://www.rae.es/rae.html) is an excellent resource for those responsible for translating materials from English to Spanish.

CULTURALLY INTELLIGENT PRINCIPAL LEADERSHIP

The successful implementation of outreach strategies to LEP families requires a schoolwide effort led by the school principal. As summarized by former principal and ESL teacher Diane Boothe (2000),

> Fostering relationships on the basis of cultural pluralism will lead to the development of a positive school environment and unlock the mysteries of the U.S. culture for non-native students. As instructional leaders, administrators must take the lead in this endeavor and be certain that all representatives of the mosaic of U.S. students have the opportunity to achieve educational success. (p. 35)

Offermann and Phan (2002) refer to this role as culturally intelligent leadership. They argue that such leadership requires that administrators (1) understand their own cultural values and biases and how these influence their expectations for themselves and others; (2) understand other cultural groups and their comparable values, biases, and expectations; and (3) adjust leadership behaviors and expectations to specific cross-cultural situations. Administrators can express this leadership by championing diversity, modeling skillful cross-cultural interactions, and mediating when cross-cultural conflict occurs (Critchfield et al., 2004).

To develop the knowledge and understanding necessary for culturally intelligent leadership, principals must reflect on their own beliefs and biases and actively challenge these biases with factual information and broad experiences. The Implicit Bias test at https://implicit.harvard.edu is a useful tool for this process. The Web-based test guides individuals through a series of activities to assess the degree of implicit preference and bias they hold for one group or another. Test takers can use this information to identify attitudes they may want to further explore and address. According to one of the test's developers, Mahzarin Banaji (Vedantam, 2005), "The implicit system is dumb. It reacts to what it sees. That is its drawback. But if we change the environment, we can change our attitudes" (p. 4).

Accordingly, principals seeking to become culturally intelligent can read widely about the cultures of their students and families and visit and participate in religious and cultural organizations that serve these families. They can also interact regularly with diverse students and families through invited lunches and principal "meet and greets." Principals can strive to hire faculty and staff who reflect the diversity of the student population and guide their schools' partnership teams in identifying, training, and supporting culturally diverse members. Through such actions, principals can lead their schools toward more inclusive and responsive partnerships with the families of LEP students.

WHY THIS MATTERS FOR PRINCIPALS

Schools are becoming more culturally and linguistically diverse. As this diversity grows, so does the LEP population. Schools must ensure that LEP students meet the same academic standards as those achieved by their English proficient counterparts. To meet this objective, schools need to partner with students' families, many of whom may be poor, employed in inflexible, low-wage jobs, limited in English proficiency, and with limited education. This requires that schools think beyond traditional means of involvement and communication to link with these families in ways that support students' success. When principals lead their schools in creating partnerships that honor diversity and demonstrate respect for families who may not speak English well, they move their schools toward realizing the spirit and intent of NCLB.

Action Steps for School Leaders

✓ Learn more about the cultures and experiences of the immigrant and LEP families in the school.

✓ Ensure that school communications are competently translated and that school activities and meetings have translators as needed.

✓ Include the school's LEP educator on the partnership team and invite that representative to share the perspective of the children and families with whom he or she works.

✓ Ensure that parent representation on the partnership team reflects the school's cultural diversity.

REFLECTION QUESTIONS

1. Are the principles of culturally intelligent leadership important for linguistically homogenous schools as well as linguistically diverse schools? Explain.

2. How might attention to the needs of LEP students and families influence the overall quality of school, family, and community partnerships in linguistically diverse schools?

6

Families Living in Poverty and School, Family, and Community Partnerships

In this chapter, we describe four strategies—employing parent liaisons, offering professional development for faculty and staff, developing relevant community partnerships, and providing integrated services—that principals can implement to create school environments that support the engagement of low-income families.

CHALLENGES FACED BY LOW-INCOME FAMILIES

One in six children in the United States lives in poverty. About 40 percent of American Indian children live in poor families, 33 percent of African

American children, 27 percent of Hispanic American children, 12 percent of Asian American children, and 10 percent of European American children (Fass & Cauther, 2007). For most of the United States, the poverty threshold for a family of four is about $20,000 (U.S. Department of Health and Human Services, 2006); however, approximately 40 percent of these families live in "severe poverty" with family incomes less than half the federal poverty threshold. About 40 percent of families living in poverty are employed (U.S. Census Bureau, 2002). Some of the unemployed poor are not working in order to care for other family members or because of illness or disability (Loprest & Acs, 1996).

Of equal concern are families that are near poverty, recently described as the "missing class" (Newman & Chen, 2007), with incomes between $20,000 and $40,000 (100 to 200 percent of the poverty threshold). According to sociologist Katherine Newman,

> There are actually almost twice as many of them [the missing class] as there are people under the poverty line—57 million in the U.S. They represent, on the one hand, an improvement, forward motion, the promise of upward mobility. But their lives are not stable. They truly are one paycheck, one lost job, one divorce or one sick child away from falling below the poverty line. (p. 1)

Low-income working parents are most likely to be employed in service occupations characterized by low earnings, inflexible work schedules, fewer opportunities for full-time employment, and limited benefits such as health insurance, paid vacations, or holidays (Newman & Chen, 2007; U.S. Department of Labor, 2005). Such work schedules make school conferences, homework help, and other expected forms of school engagement difficult if not impossible.

These employment conditions often create housing hardships, which increase rates of residential and school mobility. A report issued by the National Center for Children in Poverty (Koball, Douglas-Hall, & Chau, 2005) reported that 20 percent of children in urban, low-income families— 8.2 million—moved in 2005 seeking better homes and neighborhoods or more affordable housing. Unfortunately, the housing available to many poor and near poor families exposes children and youth to lead-based toxins and other environmental hazards compromising their social, emotional, and physical development and well-being.

Poor families are also at greater risk for homelessness. The Urban Institute reported in 2000 that, nationally, approximately half a million children aged five years old and younger experienced homelessness in the course of a year. Compared with low-income housed children, homeless children experience more health problems, developmental delays, anxiety, depression, and behavioral problems, as well as lower educational achievement (National Center on Family Homelessness, 1999). Within schools, homeless children often go unrecognized and must contend with institutional expectations of family and housing stability (Chung, 2007). Many low-income families, then, are experiencing stresses over and above those faced by families with greater economic resources. These stresses present challenges to parental involvement and home-school relations.

AVOIDING A DEFICIT PERSPECTIVE

Despite the significant stresses faced by many low-income families, these families also have strengths and coping strategies that are important to acknowledge and support to best serve children and youth. In a study of parent functioning in neighborhoods with different levels of resources, opportunities, and risks in Philadelphia, Pennsylvania, sociologist Frank Furstenberg Jr. and colleagues (2000) found that

> parenting skills, especially when measured by the standard scales that assess warmth, commitment, discipline, and control varied in only trivial ways by the quality of the neighborhood as measured by its resources and social climate. Inadequate parenting, as measured both by quantitative measures derived from the surveys of parents and children and by qualitative assessments based on indepth interviews with parents and children among a subset of thirty-five families was far more often the exception than the rule. Most parents were committed, reasonably skilled, and strongly invested in their children's welfare. The generally good quality of parenting applied to households with two resident parents as well as those with a single parent. (p. 217)

When schools and other community organizations view low-income families in their complexity, focusing realistically on their strengths and resources as well as their weaknesses and needs, families are more likely to receive services and supports that enhance their capacity to function effectively as primary caregivers. Yet, there are a variety of societal and personal factors that make it challenging for some school personnel to view poor families this way.

Negative stereotypes of poor families are reinforced through media sources and decades of research that despite ongoing challenges and revisions continues to influence educational policy and practice (see, for example, Bomer, Dworin, May, and Semington's [2008] critique of Ruby Payne's Framework for Understanding Poverty). Consequently, some educators view poor parents from a deficit perspective. According to the deficit perspective, "discrepancies in access and opportunity are explained, not by inequities, but by 'deficient' cultures and behaviors of people in poverty (and other marginalized groups)" (Gorski, 2005). A deficit perspective prevents educators from viewing poor families as partners in the education and development of children and youth and from gathering sufficient information to determine families' assets and needs and the most appropriate areas for home-school-community interactions.

For example, in their three-year ethnographic study of families living in poverty and the special education placement process, Harry, Klinger, and Hart (2005) observed:

> Certainly, the families we visited all had problems of one sort or another, but our visits to their homes introduced us to another side of the picture—the side that spoke of families' expressions of love and responsibility for their children. What we learned was that school personnel really knew very little about the families they described in the most derogatory terms. We came to understand that school personnel's views were frequently based on single pieces of information that had some basis in fact but were taken out of context to construct portraits of family identities that were far from the truth. (p. 108)

The researchers found that such views affected the behaviors of the educators, leading them to vilify parents, ignore their comments and questions during special education placement meetings, and make place-ment decisions not always in the best interest of the children and youth under their care. When schools take such an approach to families, they miss the opportunity to make a positive difference in the lives of children and adults. This chapter now turns to a discussion of strategies and resources that can help schools enhance their capacity to partner with low-income families.

A COLLABORATIVE APPROACH

When schools adopt a collaborative approach in their work with low-income families, they listen and respond to families' needs, interests, and concerns. Moreover, schools are proactive in identifying the supports and resources that educators and families require in order to work as partners in the education of children and youth. A challenge for schools, then, is to build internal resources and links to external resources to cre-ate the kinds of family supports for which Urie Bronfenbrenner, key founder of Head Start, advocated over two decades ago (Bronfenbrenner,

1985). Here, we discuss four ways in which school leaders can meet this challenge: (1) employ parent liaisons, (2) provide teacher professional development, (3) develop relevant community partnerships, and (4) provide integrated services.

Parent Liaisons

Several sources highlight the importance of parent liaisons for promoting home-school collaboration (Aparicio-Clark & Dorris, 2006; Halford, 1996; Moles, 1996; U.S. Department of Education, 2007). While the job descriptions and professional responsibilities of liaisons differ by site, a common expectation is that liaisons will help connect schools and families, especially families with the greatest needs. Schools and districts have reported positive results from their liaison programs (Kirschenbaum, 1999; Lindeman, 2002; Vulliamy & Webb, 2003), including higher student achievement and increased parent involvement (Halford, 1996; Lewis, 2000). Bilingual liaisons have been credited for increasing the involvement of families with limited English proficiency (Aparicio-Clark & Dorris, 2006).

Between 2003 and 2007, a parent liaison program developed in 2001 was the focus of a case study on district leadership for school, family, and community partnerships (see Sanders, 2008). The parent liaisons were placed in Title I schools to provide additional support to the schools' outreach efforts. The liaisons were trained by the district's family and community outreach specialist, worked part-time, and mostly had degrees in education, social work, or related fields. The district specialist found that, with appropriate training, individuals who had knowledge and skills in these professional areas could provide the broadest and most comprehensive level of support for a school's partnership efforts.

The liaisons were an important resource for families facing a variety of stresses as well as for the schools serving these families. The liaisons provided (1) direct services, (2) support for teacher outreach, (3) support for school-based partnership teams, and (4) data for program improvement. Below we describe each of these areas of support to clarify how liaisons can assist schools in partnering with poor families and others placed at risk.

Direct Services to Families Placed at Risk

Each liaison worked with approximately twelve to fifteen "focus" families in the district's lowest-performing schools. Preference was given to low-income families with children who were performing below grade level in reading and mathematics. However, other criteria included the following:

1. A family whose child had an absentee rate of 20 percent or greater

2. A family whose child had inconsistent rates of homework completion

3. A family that appeared to be disenfranchised or alienated from the school

Two parent liaisons described their support for focus families in the following ways:

> As parent liaisons, we give parents the tools they need to communicate with teachers and administrators. It might begin with our accompanying a parent to a parent-teacher conference and being there with that parent and sitting there with that parent. Eventually they'll be able to go by themselves.

> We are maybe the very first people that these parents are meeting who say to them, "You know, we believe in you. We support you; we know that you just need a little help right now."

Survey results from thirty focus families, while not statistically representative of all focus families in the district, corroborated these liaison reports. Focus families rated the liaisons positively. Liaisons were rated particularly high on being available to families when they needed them, on providing services to meet family needs, and on overall satisfaction with the assistance provided.

Support for Teacher Outreach

Due to lack of experience and professional development, many teachers—regardless of age and ethnicity—do not have the skills, knowledge, and dispositions necessary to effectively communicate and partner with low-income families. One liaison, a former teacher, described the gap in home-school communication in the following way: "As educators, we often want to get out our message—that is what we are focused on. We are not focused on the receivers of the message, the families. They need support in hearing the message so that we can both support the child."

Liaisons in this study supported teachers in reaching out to the families of diverse students by modeling outreach strategies that helped build teachers' capacity for partnerships. They also acted as cultural interpreters, helping teachers better understand students' traditions, modes of expression, and experiences outside the school. By doing so, they helped teachers reach out to families who might otherwise have been pushed to the margins of the school community. According to one liaison, "I've had teachers tell me I've made a difference, and that is a good thing to hear."

Support for School–Based Partnership Teams

Parent liaisons also worked with school partnership teams to conduct schoolwide activities that were accessible and relevant to the families of all students. During the course of the study, partnership team members, including the school principals, underscored the important role parent liaisons played in providing family support, implementing family outreach, and garnering greater parent involvement for students' school success.

For example, based on the insights and perspectives offered by the parent liaison, one partnership school decided to hold a family reading activity in the meeting room of an apartment building where many students and families resided. Another school decided to implement activities specifically for Hispanic families because their attendance at school-wide events was low. These well-attended activities, which created a safe space for Latino families to learn more about school programs, share information and concerns, as well as network with other families and school personnel, were led by the parent liaison, who spoke fluent English and Spanish.

Data for Program Improvement

Each liaison used Epstein's framework of six types of involvement to complete a weekly activity report that described her focus family and school outreach activities. Liaisons also collected achievement and attendance data for targeted students in the focus families. Ongoing assessment data were collected at the beginning of the school year and at the end of each grading period to track student progress over the school year.

In addition to tracking student achievement data, parent liaisons and school-based partnership teams collected and analyzed demographic data not only for students but also for their families and communities. Parent liaisons, in particular, were expected to develop deep understanding and knowledge of their focus families so that they could provide "wrap-around" services to help these families better support their children's learning and general well-being. Parent liaisons collected data on families' financial, health, and emotional needs and concerns. These data helped identify additional resources and actions that could aid the families.

These liaisons illustrate the potential all liaisons have for any school. Through telephone calls, home visits, school meetings, informal conversations, and authentic expressions of care and respect, liaisons can assist families in meeting their parenting obligations, help bridge the home-school divide, and expand the social networks of low-income families. While social networks that include close ties with other parents and professionals are commonly seen among middle-class families, they are less visible in working class and poor families (Horvat, Weininger, & Lareau, 2003). Liaisons can disrupt this class-based pattern of parental networks and help increase the social capital of low-income families.

Teacher Professional Development

Activities that build the capacity of teachers to strengthen relationships with low-income families and families viewed as "hard to reach" also are important. McDermott (2008) emphasized the need for teachers as well as parents to be viewed as developing adults who require support in reaching their capacity as caring, empathetic stakeholders within school, family, and community partnerships. In addition, NCLB legislation requires schools to provide professional development for families and staff on how to "work together productively" (National Coalition for Parent Involvement in Education [NCPIE], 2004, p. 4).

Professional development topics for teachers and staff should be based on school personnel's needs and concerns. A variety of formats can be used, including workshops, study groups, and action research projects. Topics might include cultural proficiency, conflict management, poverty and homelessness in the United States, home-school collaboration, and parenting in the twenty-first century. Through such professional development, teachers will be given opportunities to reflect on their beliefs, assumptions, and practices as they relate to their students' families (see Box 6.1). Individuals who can help support such professional development include school and district specialists (e.g., counselors, social workers, and psychologists), university faculty, and community organizers.

Box 6.1   An Educator's Reflection on Bias

The readings we did on the bias that colors the interactions between teachers and their parents (especially low-income parents) brought the idea of bias to the forefront of my mind. Since those readings, I have witnessed my own bias in my interactions with parents (where I once believed there was none). For example, I had to call home about a critical issue concerning the personal safety of a student. I reached her mother, a woman who has never come to school or answered a phone call from school for this child's entire educational career. I believed that her lack of attendance was a demonstration of her apathy toward her daughter. When I called home and the mother answered the phone, I felt a change in my tone and deliverance of my message. I was callous when discussing the situation that occurred at school and used a monotone voice. I sounded as if I was performing a perfunctory duty and that this phone call wasn't important.

As the phone call progressed, I could hear this mother's concern for her child, and I was deeply ashamed at the way I had shared my information. This interaction reminded me that my behavior affects my relationships, that there is more to a situation than I can see, and that parents deserve respect—period. This interaction along with the readings emphasized the critical need for teachers, myself included, to reflect on their stereotyped beliefs. As I reflect on my beliefs and behaviors, I know I will change.

Community Partnerships

Schools can also work with a variety of community partners to provide a multitude of needed resources for low-income families (see Table 6.1). Through parent surveys, liaison reports, and other forms of communication, schools can assess their parents' needs and connect with community organizations to respond to those needs. Through simple and complex family-centered activities (see Figure 6.1) at the school or at conveniently located community organizations, schools can ensure that families have access to food banks, parent or grandparent support groups, drug and alcohol recovery programs, job-training and GED programs, family counseling services, housing programs, and information on school programs, requirements, and expectations (see Sanders, 2005). Schools can also offer after-school programs to provide students with the adult-supervised enrichment activities that have been linked to higher student achievement and increased well-being (Clark, 2002; Heath & McLaughlin, 1996) (see Box 6.2).

Table 6.1   Community Partners and Foci of Partnership Activities

Activity Focus	*Community Partners*
Student centered (e.g., student awards, student incentives, scholarships, student trips, tutors, mentors, job shadowing, and other services and products for students)	Businesses/corporations (e.g., local businesses, national corporations and franchises) Universities and educational institutions (e.g., colleges and universities, high schools, and other educational institutions)
Family centered (e.g., parent workshops, family fun nights, GED and other adult education classes, parent incentives and rewards, counseling and other forms of assistance) School centered (e.g., equipment and materials, beautification and repair, teacher incentives and awards, funds for school events and programs, office and classroom assistance)	Health care organizations (e.g., hospitals, health care centers, mental health facilities, health departments, health foundations, and associations) Government and military agencies (e.g., fire departments, police departments, chamber of commerce, city council, other local and state government agencies and departments) National service and volunteer organizations (e.g., Rotary Club, Lions Club, Kiwanis Club, VISTA, Concerned Black Men, Inc., Shriners, Boys and Girls Scouts, YMCA, United Way, Americorp, Urban League, etc.)

(Continued)

Table 6.1 (Continued)

Activity Focus	Community Partners
Community centered (e.g., community beautification, student exhibits and performances, charity, and other outreach)	Faith-based organizations (e.g., churches, mosques, synagogues, other religious organizations, and charities) Senior citizens organizations (e.g., nursing homes, senior volunteer and service organizations) Cultural and recreational institutions (e.g., zoos, museums, libraries, recreational centers) Media organizations (e.g., local newspapers, radio stations, cable networks, etc.) Sports franchises and associations (e.g., minor and major league sports teams, NBA, NCAA, etc.) Other community organizations (e.g., fraternities, sororities, foundations, neighborhood associations, political, alumni, etc.) Community individuals (e.g., individual volunteers from the surrounding school community)

Source: Adapted from Sanders, M. G. (2001). A study of the role of "community" in comprehensive school, family, and community partnership programs. *The Elementary School Journal, 102*(1), 19–34.

Figure 6.1   Community Partnerships: Range of Complexity

Simple Partnerships	Complex Partnerships
• Short term • Unidirectional exchange • Low level of interaction • Limited planning	• Long term • Bi- or multidirectional exchange • High level of interaction • Extensive planning and coordination
Examples: incentives for awards programs, donation of school materials/supplies	Examples: full-service community schools; professional development schools

Box 6.2   After-School Enrichment Program

Frederick Law Olmsted School #64/56, Buffalo, New York

Parents often spend a great deal of time, energy, and money trying to find constructive after-school activities for their children. At Frederick Law Olmsted School, however, that is no longer necessary. The After-School Enrichment program provides an hour of creative activities and experiences every day, while furthering the school's goals and preparing students for required tests. During two six-week sessions, about 100 Olmsted students participated in crafts, yoga, and cooking, as well as many other fun and educational activities. Parents and community partners of the two-site elementary-middle school contributed heavily to the successful program:

- The Explore and More Children's Museum conducted hands-on, culture-themed crafts activities.
- The Himalaya Institute provided a yoga instructor.
- The Darlene Ceglia Dance Project taught hip hop dancing, while the Buffalo Inner-City Ballet prepared beginning dancers well enough to perform in *The Nutcracker* at Shea's Performing Arts Center, downtown Buffalo's largest theater.
- Two professional chefs taught fifth and sixth graders how to read recipes and safely prepare a variety of dishes.

More than 20 parents volunteered their time and talents. One parent who works as an art teacher in another district came in on her day off to teach pop-up bookmaking; another taught knitting—using rhymes to take the students through the steps. A group of parents brought in board games for students to play with their friends. Although Olmsted had many reasons to create an after-school enrichment program, two topped the list—reinforcing the skills needed to do well on the ELA and Terra Nova assessments and increasing the role of parents and community partners to meet some of the goals of the school's Comprehensive School Education Plan.

The activities the Action Team for Partnerships (ATP) designed for the enrichment program support the learning skills necessary for improvement on those required tests. The ATP advertised the after-school program through Olmsted's weekly parent information packet, as well as through phone calls and e-mails. To cover costs, the school charged $10 per student for each six-week session. The fee was waived for families who could not afford to pay it. The level of participation and attendance showed that the after-school program met a need and also tapped the significant resources available to the school. The program created a greater

(Continued)

(Continued)

sense of community and pride in the school. Olmsted also furthered its mission of fostering higher-level thinking skills, creative problem solving, and habits that support life-long learning through the differentiated learning experiences provided.

Kate Willoughby, ATP Co-Chair

Source: Brownstein, J., Maushard, M., Robinson, J., Greenfeld, M., & Hutchins, D. (Eds.). (2006). *Promising partnership practices, 2006*. Baltimore, MD: National Network of Partnership Schools. Reprinted with permission, © 2006 National Network of Partnership Schools, Johns Hopkins University.

Schools can also partner with individuals and organizations in the community to address the needs of specific populations. The partnership team in a large high school in Cleveland, Ohio (see Sanders & Lewis, 2004, for the full study), for example, created WHEW (Women Helping Educate Women) to support their parenting teens and other mothers and daughters in the school. WHEW aimed to provide girls and their mothers with information to make positive choices in their academic and personal lives. Community speakers provided information on a number of topics of relevance to these families, including HIV/AIDS prevention and management, parenting skills, positive family communication, academic and career opportunities, and educational and community support for high school females, especially teen mothers.

Schools across the nation have also been investing time in creating community resource manuals for their families. These manuals describe local community organizations that provide essential services to families. They can be organized around important issues such as housing, health, family counseling and support, food and nutrition, out-of-school-time learning opportunities for children and youth, and adult education and job training. Community partners that might be included are local chapters of the Salvation Army, YMCA, and other service organizations; local churches and religious organizations; homeless and battered women shelters; food banks; local utility companies; and community medical clinics. Community resource manuals are most useful when they include names and contact information for individuals who will be accessible to parents and able to help them secure needed services. Developing and updating such resource manuals becomes an important and ongoing school partnership activity.

Integrated Services

Integrated services are another important way that schools can ensure they are providing services that can support family functioning before crises occur. They are also an important way to ease the fragmentation of services faced by many low-income families who do not have the resources to manage them. Many poor families are without personal transportation and have to make several stops by public transportation or walking to access health and dental care, attend school-based activities, and receive housing and food assistance. Community schools providing integrated services or "one stop" shopping are promising ways to ease the burdens and stress experienced by these families; to promote coordination among service providers; and to enhance families' health, well-being, and engagement in their children's learning. Community schools have been linked to higher student attendance and achievement, increased parental involvement, more positive school climates, higher teacher satisfaction, and improved community relations (Blank, Melaville, & Shah, 2003).

When describing these schools, Blank, Melaville, and Shah (2003) wrote:

> Using public schools as hubs, community schools knit together inventive, enduring relationships among educators, families, volunteers and community partners. Health and social service agencies, family support groups, youth development organizations, institutions of higher education, community organizations, businesses, and civic and faith-based groups all play a part. (p. 2)

Community schools are thus better positioned than traditional public schools to address the social, emotional, physical, and intellectual needs of children and families living in poverty. The coordination of these services, however, requires strong principal leadership that begins with a clear vision of how the school can effectively integrate these partners.

Although some principals have well-developed visions for integrated services, these visions are often created without input from key stakeholders. An imposed vision for a community school is a contradiction that often results in failed or poorly executed efforts (Decker, Decker, & Brown, 2007). Principals, then, should first identify a planning committee composed of key school, family, and community representatives. These stakeholders may include, but not be limited to, school board members, community organizers and leaders, parents, teachers, students in the upper grades, business leaders, and district leaders for family and community engagement. The school's partnership team can act as the planning committee, a subcommittee of the partnership team can be formed and additional members added to form the planning committee, or a separate committee can be formed. In any case, it is important that goals, timelines, and rules of engagement are established for this stage of the process.

The planning team should construct a collaborative vision for the community school. The vision should be based on as much information or data as possible to identify school, family, community, and student needs. Needs assessments can be conducted through parent/teacher/student surveys, community meetings, focus groups with targeted populations, or a combination of these methods. Needs assessments should seek information such as academic and nonacademic goals for students; students' out-of-school-time activities and needs; families' childcare, health, employment, and educational needs; and other information that will help craft the community school vision.

This requires time because collaboration as a process cannot be rushed. According to Gray (1991), "The importance of process cannot be overemphasized in planning and conducting successful collaborations. Good-faith efforts to undertake collaboration are often derailed because the parties are not skilled in the process and because insufficient attention is given to designing and managing a constructive process" (p. 93).

After the vision has been established, the planning committee must secure space and funding. Some schools use extra space within their buildings; others use nearby buildings, such as community centers, churches, or other available spaces that are either rented or donated; still others build new buildings or purchase buildings close to the school. Grant funds, such as those available through the 21st Century Learning Communities program, private foundations, affordable fees for service, and Title I funds, are also likely sources of financing, as well as Medicaid funds if school clinics are established. The total funding needed, however, will depend largely on the types of services provided (Dryfoos & Maguire, 2002).

Once funding has been secured, the vision for the community school should be widely disseminated, and opportunities for additional input from and dialogue with school, family, and community members scheduled. Although time consuming, two-way communication increases the likelihood of greater buy-in from key constituents. Principals, as school and community leaders, should be at the forefront of these dissemination and communication efforts.

Principals, then, must be or become adept at public relations. According to Decker, Decker, and Brown (2007),

> Simply put, school PR is not about letting everyone make decisions. It is about letting families and community members know that their input is valued and taken seriously, and that they are welcome and needed. How well a school leader is able to meet the school PR challenge will depend in large part on his or her ability to communicate—communicate to inform and develop high morale among staff members, communicate to build a team with families focused on the education of their children, and communicate to develop public support within the community and among elected leaders. (p. 168)

After buy-in has been established, a coordinator must be identified and hired. The coordinator then becomes a member of the planning committee, which will also oversee the implementation and evaluation of the integrated services provided. The coordinator is responsible for the daily management of the services and therefore must communicate regularly and effectively with the principal, community partners, the school improvement or management team, the PTA or other parent organizations, and others as needed. The coordinator also is responsible for identifying and replacing community partners as needed and as guided by the school's vision, identifying and scheduling needed facilities and helping to identify potential sources of funding and applying for those funds. According to Blank, Melaville, and Shah (2003), "The coordinator . . . can greatly improve the range, quality and coherence of community school activities while increasing the time the principal and other school staff can devote to instruction and learning" (p. 54). For additional information on developing community schools, visit the Coalition for Community Schools at http://www.communityschools.org.

WHY THIS MATTERS FOR PRINCIPALS

A stated goal of NCLB is to close the achievement gap that exists between low-income students and their more economically affluent peers. To achieve this objective, principals must focus on the needs of these students as well as their families. All families face challenges. Poor families, however, face greater challenges due to their limited financial resources.

When principals who serve poor families recognize their challenges and work to address them, they increase these families' opportunities and capacity to become more engaged in their children's education. When they do not, engagement is likely to remain limited as families grapple with the often overwhelming responsibilities of meeting their basic needs. By engaging in practices that facilitate the involvement of poor families and families in the missing class, principals can bridge the gulf between home and school that limits the potentially transformative impact of education. The final section of this book first explores the issue of partnership program evaluation, and then offers concluding thoughts about the implementation and maintenance of coordinated programs of school, family, and community partnerships.

Action Steps for School Leaders

✓ Model and set as an expectation for faculty and staff unbiased, respectful communication and interaction with all students and families.

✓ Develop relationships with local service providers and community organizations to share information about and coordinate efforts to serve children and families.

✓ Ensure that parent representatives, regardless of socioeconomic background, are provided the training and information required to be fully engaged members of the school's partnership team.

REFLECTION QUESTIONS

1. In 1995, Joyce Epstein wrote, "The way schools care about children is reflected in the way schools care about the children's families." Do you agree or disagree with this statement? Explain your position.

2. What do you believe is the primary function of schools? Given the function(s) you identified, which, if any, strategy suggested in this chapter would be appropriate to implement? Explain your answer.

3. What do you believe are the costs and benefits of implementing strategies described in this chapter in schools with significant percentages of students from low-income backgrounds?

PART III

Maximizing Outcomes

7

Evaluating Programs of School, Family, and Community Partnerships

This chapter discusses the process of program evaluation, from establishing clarity about the purpose of the evaluation to disseminating results to key stakeholders. Well-designed evaluations help principals examine the partnership efforts at their schools, understand how these efforts affect students and families, and determine how they might be improved over time.

Too often in education, decisions about whether or how to implement a school program are not informed by any type of evaluation. Evaluation is the systematic collection and examination of data to help make decisions that can, among other things, help *prove* and *improve* a program's effectiveness (Kellogg Foundation, 1998; Muraskin, 1993). The process of program evaluation includes planning, collecting, coding, and analyzing data and presenting the findings (Muraskin, 1993). Although in some cases a school or district might contract with an outside person or group to help conduct an evaluation, many times a useful evaluation can be done internally.

The primary goal of this chapter is to help principals think about and prepare to evaluate partnership programs at their schools. Because the topic of program evaluation is so vast, this chapter serves only as an introduction. It covers the topics of evaluation planning, data collection, and presentation of findings. Readers interested in issues pertaining to data coding and analysis are encouraged to consult some of the resources described in this chapter.

There are many reasons for evaluating an individual school project or program. A good evaluation can help determine the effectiveness of a program, document that a program's goals have been met, provide information about the implementation of a program, and illustrate areas where a program can improve. Research suggests that program evaluations are beneficial to school, family, and community partnership efforts. Schools that conduct evaluations of their partnership programs are more likely to see their programs improve from one year to the next than are schools that do not (Epstein et al., 2002; Sheldon & Van Voorhis, 2004).

In addition to understanding the strengths and weaknesses of current partnership activities, conducting an evaluation can help legitimize efforts to involve families and communities. By engaging in the process of program evaluation, "the evaluator is essentially sending a message that the program is a serious effort, worth the time and resources that it takes to evaluate" (Weiss, 1998, p. 25). Principals and school leaders trying to build momentum for a partnership program may find that conducting an evaluation of current partnership efforts helps build consensus about the importance of this work. Clarity in the reasons behind an evaluation is important because it is one of the determinants of how an evaluation is conducted.

PLANNING AN EVALUATION

Before the first piece of information is collected and long before any conclusions can be drawn, it is vital to think through and plan an evaluation strategy. Clarity about the long-term goals of a program and the various steps needed to achieve those goals is necessary if an evaluation is to address important aspects of the program (Weiss, 1995). The first step in the evaluation process, then, is to understand the program's underlying theory and assumptions.

Clarity of program goals and processes can be achieved in a variety of ways. Two methods commonly used are logic models and theory of change frameworks. Both approaches are designed to make explicit the assumptions about how a program and its accompanying activities will help an organization achieve its desired goals. In the context of partnerships, these tools will help program leaders identify and articulate the organizational and outreach activities to be implemented, as well as the goals and outcomes these features are expected to achieve.

Logic models and theory of change frameworks help make public in a clear format the resources and theories driving program activities. These tools allow individuals to communicate the purposes, resources, practices, and results of a program in one or two pages. After completing these exercises, individuals working with the program should be able to communicate better with each other as well as with those external to the program (e.g., those being served by or overseeing the program). Each of these planning tools is discussed separately.

Logic Models

There is no single way to construct a logic model, though every model should identify a program's available resources, activities, outputs, and expected outcomes (see Figure 7.1); in other words, it should explain the things the program needs, the activities the program conducts, the services the program provides, and the changes the program seeks to achieve. Through describing each of these aspects of the program and determining the most suitable type of evaluation, an executable plan can be constructed.

The first step in creating a logic model for a program is to identify needed resources. These are often referred to as *inputs* to the program. For a partnership program, the inputs may include staff and volunteers, meeting space and time, financial support, in-kind support from community partners, and other resources that allow individuals to plan and carry out partnership program activities.

The next step is to identify the activities of the program. These are the things that need to be done to provide partnership services. Examples of partnership program activities might include creating a partnership team, conducting regular partnership team meetings, developing a one-year action plan of goal-oriented partnership practices, and communicating about partnership activities with the larger school community (Epstein et al., 2002). These activities are most likely to be related to organizational aspects of the school that allow staff to effectively involve families and community partners.

The third step is to identify program outputs. Outputs are the services delivered to achieve short- and long-term goals. In regards to a program of school, family, and community partnerships, program outputs are the specific family and community involvement activities being implemented. Examples of these kinds of activities might include hosting family workshops, communicating with families through newsletters, having parents volunteer to help the school, and collaborating with local businesses to provide incentives for students. These are the activities that will directly connect the school and teachers to students' families and community leaders.

The fourth step involves identifying the outcomes expected as a result of the program's outputs. These outcomes are the changes the school community hopes and expects to bring about as a result of program services. Outcomes

Figure 7.1 Logic Model Template

Inputs		Activities	Outputs		Outcomes		
					Short Term	Mid-range	Long Term
What we invest:		What we do:	Services we provide:		Expected short-term effects:	Expected mid-range effects:	Expected long-term effects:

should be organized according to changes expected in the short term as well as in the long term. For some programs, it may even be sensible to consider listing some mid-range outcomes.

In clarifying the outcomes of a program, some important guidelines should be kept in mind. For example, the outcomes attributed to a program need to be achievable and within its sphere of influence. For a program of school, family, and community partnerships, a reasonable outcome might be to improve rates of student homework completion over the course of the school year. An unrealistic outcome would be to provide families in need with gainful employment so that they can provide more resources at home for their children. Whereas improved homework completion rates might be achieved through better communication with families, the latter outcome, while laudable, is beyond a school's capacity.

Typically, logic models are written as a series of "If-Then" statements. A good check for a completed logic model is that it conforms with the following reasoning:

1. If the inputs are available, then the program will be able to complete the necessary activities.

2. If the necessary activities are implemented, then the program will be able to deliver the services listed in the output section.

3. If the program has delivered the desired services, then changes can occur to realize the short-term goals.

4. If the short-term goals are achieved, then the long-terms goals of the program can be achieved.

The extent to which the logic model satisfactorily meets these If-Then statements and accurately portrays the partnership program determines the program's readiness for the next steps in the evaluation.

Theory of Change Frameworks

A theory of change is a way to describe the various steps of a program that will lead to a long-term goal and the set of assumptions that explain why these program activities should produce desired outcomes (see Figure 7.2). Anderson (2005) has described a theory of change as "the product of a series of critical thinking exercises that provides a comprehensive picture of the early- and intermediate-term changes in a given community that are needed to reach a long-term goal articulated by the community" (see Harris, 2005, p. 12). A theory of change helps guide the evaluation of a school's partnership program by identifying a long-term goal and then mapping backward toward the preconditions necessary to achieve that goal. It also identifies how intervention activities are designed to create the preconditions necessary to realize the long-term goal.

Figure 7.2   Theory of Change Template

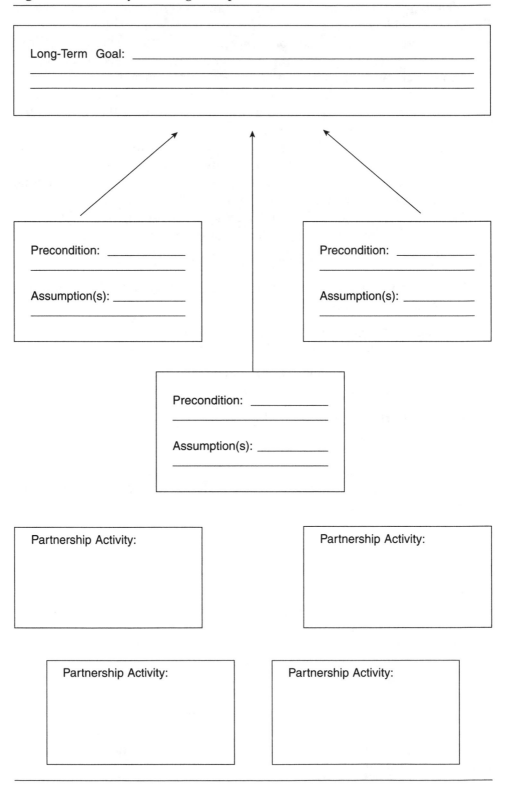

The first step in constructing a theory of change is to identify one or more long-term goals of the program. These goals need to be specific. Any generic terms used to describe the program or its goals need to be defined. School programs, for example, should not list "improved student achievement" as a goal but should specify the types of achievement (e.g., grade, test score, grade level promotion, etc.) and levels of expected improvement. Next, participants need to map out the preconditions—building blocks or requirements—to the long-term goal (Anderson, 2005). These are conditions that must exist for the long-term goal to be met. It is important to make as explicit as possible assumptions about why a precondition can create the long-term goal.

The second step in constructing a theory of change is to backward map preconditions and assumptions until an explanation is reached of what the program does, what it aims to accomplish, and how the sequence of achievements is expected to occur. At this step of backward mapping, what were preconditions should be thought of as outcomes. Identifying the procedures and conditions that make the new outcomes (previously our preconditions) possible is the primary goal. At this stage, then, it is important to list program activities that help create the preconditions for the various goals.

The third step in the creation of a theory of change is to draw connections between program activities, preconditions, and outcomes. Because not all preconditions or assumptions are associated with every outcome, evaluators and program partners should draw lines, literally, that illustrate the connections between program activities, preconditions, and specific outcomes.

The theory of change process is expected to involve multiple stakeholders associated with a program. For a partnership program, it may be helpful for the partnership team and other interested parties to brainstorm answers to some basic questions about the program. These questions require individuals to identify the who, what, where, and whys of a given program. While brainstorming answers to these questions, gaps or inconsistencies in peoples' thinking about what and how a program is expected to achieve should surface (see Box 7.1).

Box 7.1   Guiding Questions to Create Your Theory of Change

Together with colleagues, brainstorm responses to the following questions to clarify program goals and activities and begin to construct a theory of change to guide partnership evaluation.

1. Who will be affected by the program?

2. What actions will the program undertake?

3. Where will the actions take place?

4. What outcomes is the program expected to produce?

There is not a single best method to follow for constructing a theory of change; however, all methods should begin by listing long-term outcomes and then diagramming how these outcomes are a function of preconditions and assumptions that guide the program.

Whether an evaluation begins by developing a theory of change or a logic model depends on the preferences of the evaluators and persons involved with the program. Both frameworks are strategies for making explicit the rationale for a program and the mechanisms by which specific activities will help achieve specific and general outcomes. They make public the program theory. Once there is consensus on the program theory, the framework can be used to guide data collection and help identify which types of information are needed (see Box 7.2).

Box 7.2   Helpful Resources

Theory of Change

www.theoryofchange.org. This Web site is a good source of information and guidance for using a theory of change approach to conduct program evaluation.

Harvard Family Research Project. *The Evaluation Exchange, 11*(2) (2005).

Logic Model

Useable Knowledge, LLC. This nonprofit evaluation and consulting firm has a very easy-to-understand presentation about logic models. The link to the online presentation is http://www.usablellc.net/Logic%20Model%20(Online)/Presentation_Files/index.html.

COLLECTING DATA

With a solid understanding of the partnership program, its goals, and the activities expected to realize those goals, it is now important to consider issues related to data collection. The first step in this stage of the evaluation process is to consider the purpose of the evaluation and develop a data collection plan aligned with that purpose. Ultimately, the goal(s) of the evaluation will determine the data that are collected.

There are three dimensions or types of evaluation, although an evaluation can have more than one purpose (see Box 7.3). Evaluations can focus on program processes, program outcomes, or program impact (Muraskin, 1993). Process evaluations describe and assess program materials and examine the implementation of program activities. Outcome evaluations focus on the immediate impact of a program on participants. Finally, impact evaluations identify long-term outcomes that can be attributed to a program. Whether the focus of an evaluation is on processes, outcomes, or impacts is based on local needs and available resources.

Box 7.3   Three Types of Evaluation

Process evaluation: Describes and assesses program materials and activities. Examination of materials developed and the implementation of activities are important characteristics of this type of evaluation.

Outcome evaluation: Assesses program achievements and effects. Examines the immediate or direct effects of a program on participants' knowledge, attitudes, and/or behaviors.

Impact evaluation: Examines the long-term and unintended effects of a program. These evaluations might include analyses into whether or not program effects were sustained over time.

Source: L. Muraskin. (1993). *Understanding evaluation: The way to better prevention programs.* Washington, DC: U.S. Department of Education.

A partnership program, no matter how new or experienced, can benefit from conducting one of these types of evaluations. For schools just beginning to develop a partnership program, conducting a process evaluation may be most helpful. This approach will enable school leaders to systematically review the organizational aspects of the program as well as the degree to which the involvement activities are reaching students' families. More experienced leaders, that is, those running programs that are better organized and have greater family participation, might conduct an outcome or impact evaluation to determine if and how the activities that are conducted affect parents and/or students. The needs of the school and the amount of program experience, together, should help determine the type of evaluation to carry out.

Identifying Indicators

After a good logic model or theory of change framework has been developed, it can be used to help identify what needs to be measured in a program evaluation. Program theory (logic model or theory of change) helps "pinpoint the events, activities, relationships, and outcomes that are central to the initiative's success" (Reisner, 2004). The proper indicator, or the measurable variable that represents an outcome of interest, will reflect the core elements of the program theory and the purpose of the evaluation.

For example, questions about how well the partnership program and involvement activities are being implemented are best answered through a process evaluation. Useful indicators for measuring partnership program implementation often focus on organizational processes and on how well family and community involvement activities were implemented or attended. To identify important indicators of program implementation, ask questions such as, Were planned activities conducted? Did the activities reflect their intended purpose? Were the activities well organized? Were responsibilities for implementing the program activities fairly and efficiently shared? These questions should help identify some meaningful indicators of activity execution and quality and organizational functioning.

Understanding the effect(s) of a partnership program on teachers, parents, and/or students requires an outcome or impact evaluation. Review the program's logic model or theory of change and ask who is expected to change, what is expected to change, and how might one know if the change(s) occurred? Answers to these questions will help identify the necessary information to collect as well as the best possible sources for that information.

More often than not, evaluation of a school's partnership program will be a process evaluation. For principals interested in evaluating some of the ideas contained within this book, a process evaluation might focus on the degree to which there is teamwork, the degree to which the school is implementing a wide range of family and community involvement activities, and the degree to which often overlooked populations are being reached. Certainly one group of people from whom to collect information about the level of teamwork on partnerships throughout the school are those on the partnership team. However, it might also be useful to collect data from individuals (teachers, parents, and students) who are not on the team to assess the degree to which program activities and ideas are integrated throughout the school community.

At least some reports about the implementation of family involvement activities should come from teachers, administrators, and family members. With families, however, it is important to ask those highly involved at the school *and* those less-often present at the school. Gathering data from the fullest range of individuals within the school community will provide the most comprehensive perspective on the degree to which the partnership program is successfully connecting to families.

In the event that an outcome evaluation is desired, indicators associated with changes in people's behaviors or attitudes are most commonly needed. For most schools, evaluations of the effects of partnership programs should focus on short-term outcomes. Outcomes might include changes in levels or types of family involvement, changes in student attitudes about school, or possibly changes in student attendance. Evaluation of short-term effects is important because long-term goals and outcomes are often the direct result of short-term goals and preconditions.

Impact evaluations are often difficult to implement. This form of evaluation requires sophisticated knowledge about project design and research methods and statistics, as well as high levels of resources. Rarely are these conditions available to schools and partnership program leaders. Most often, impact evaluations are conducted by a third-party individual or group external to the organization implementing the program.

If an outcome or impact evaluation is desired, consider levels of measurement when determining appropriate indicators of success. Do not try to assess changes in people who did not receive the program or at aggregated levels that should not experience change. For example, trying to demonstrate the impact of a series of family literacy workshops that involved thirty families will be extremely difficult if the indicator you are using is the percentage of students at a school that passed a standardized reading achievement test. In even the best-case scenario, it is unlikely that changes in thirty families will shift levels of reading test performance across the entire student body. Instead, an impact study of the family literacy workshops should focus on changes in the reading behaviors, attitudes, and, possibly, achievement of students and families who participated in the workshops.

Determining How to Collect Data

Planning what data to collect and how to collect it is critical to any program evaluation. First and foremost, there is no single "best" type or method of collecting data for an evaluation. The type of data and method of collection should correspond to the goals of the evaluation. Once indicators have been identified, the next step is to plan how best to get that information.

Although we typically think about surveys when discussing research and evaluation, there are several other ways to collect data. Each of these methods has its own strengths and weaknesses (see Table 7.1). In many cases, survey data is not the best method for gathering data and conducting an evaluation. Collecting survey data, typically, is considered appropriate when information is required from a very large number of individuals and if the evaluation requires the use of statistical comparisons across settings or over time. The disadvantages of using surveys, however, are that they reduce your ability to learn new information about a program, they require at least some knowledge of statistics, and often individuals do not return surveys because of a lack of clarity in the survey questions or the impersonal nature of this data collection method.

An alternative data collection strategy is to conduct one-on-one interviews. This method addresses some of the disadvantages of surveys, but it has its own limitations. Interviewing individuals is a strong method of data collection when the evaluator wants in-depth information about a topic or when participants' perceptions are of greatest interest. Interviews, however, are time consuming and cannot provide a perspective on the degree to which a perception is shared throughout a large community or group. In the end, the decision about which type of data to collect should be driven by the purposes of the evaluation.

Table 7.1   Methods to Collect Information

Method	Overall Purpose	Advantages	Disadvantages
Questionnaires, surveys, checklists	To quickly and/or easily get a lot of information from people in a nonthreatening way	• Can complete anonymously • Inexpensive to administer • Easy to compare and analyze • Administer to many people • Can get lots of data • Usually, many sample questionnaires already exist	• Might not get careful feedback • Wording can bias responses • Impersonal • May need sampling expert • Doesn't get full story
Interviews	To fully understand someone's impressions or experiences or learn more about their answers to questionnaires	• Get full range and depth of information • Develops relationships with client • Can be flexible with client	• Can take much time • Can be hard to analyze and compare • Can be costly • Interviewer can bias responses
Observation	To gather accurate information about how a program actually operates, particularly about processes	• View operations of a program as they are occurring • Can adapt to events as they occur	• Can be difficult to interpret seen behavior • Can be complex to categorize observations • Can influence behavior of participants • Can be expensive
Focus groups	To explore a topic in depth through group discussion, e.g., about reactions to an experience or suggestion, understanding common complaints, etc.; useful in evaluation and marketing	• Quickly and reliably get common impressions • Can be efficient way to get much range and depth of information in a short time • Can convey key information about programs	• Can be hard to analyze responses • Need good facilitator for safety and disclosure • Difficult to schedule 6–8 people together

PRESENTING THE FINDINGS

An equally important decision during the evaluation of a partnership program is what to do with the information gained. How to report the findings of an evaluation depends on the intended audience (Muraskin, 1993). Often, evaluations result in a written report that presents the specific findings, as well as a summary of the findings and conclusions. Oral presentations of the insights gained, however, can be an equally important and meaningful way of disseminating evaluation findings.

Results of a program evaluation should be presented to and discussed by colleagues and program staff. Although school principals do not need to be in charge of evaluating the partnership program at their schools, they should be given the opportunity to examine the findings and contribute to any final written report. Principals should also consider other important stakeholders with whom to share the evaluation, such as teachers, parents, and district leaders.

The results of a program evaluation should be presented objectively. Almost inevitably, there will be positive findings and findings that may not present the program in the most favorable light. Both kinds of findings should be included in any final report or presentation of the evaluation. Also, the evaluation report should not portray the results as though they are definitive findings on the program; rather, the findings should be reported as tools the staff can use for examining strengths and weaknesses.

The following guidelines by Muraskin (1993) can help construct a written or oral report of the evaluation's findings:

- State why the evaluation was conducted.
- State the questions asked as part of the evaluation.
- State the purpose of the program that was evaluated.
- Indicate what was hoped to be learned as a result of conducting the evaluation.
- Share the highlights of the results.
- Describe the implications of the findings for the program's continuation and improvement.
- When appropriate, provide recommendations to improve future evaluations.

WHY THIS MATTERS FOR PRINCIPALS

The evaluation of a partnership program, or any school program, is a strategy for discovering ways to improve effectiveness. Frameworks like the logic model or theory of change can help principals and partnership leaders understand what, why, and how the program is expected to benefit teachers, families, and students. Based on this understanding, plans for data collection and analysis can be made and enacted. Information gained through the evaluation process should clarify which aspects of the partnership program are working well, which components need improvement, and what results have been achieved. This information cannot be gained or communicated to others without systematic examination of a school's partnership program.

Action Steps for School Leaders

✓ Identify a committee on the partnership team to coordinate and oversee program evaluation.

✓ Share key partnership program objectives and results at parent meetings, other appropriate school gatherings, and in home-school communications such as school newsletters.

REFLECTION QUESTIONS

1. When might a school want to conduct a process evaluation? An outcome evaluation? An impact evaluation?

2. What might be some useful strategies for collecting information from parents about a school's family and community involvement activities?

3. What are some short-term and long-term outcomes you expect from the family and community involvement activities that occur at your school?

Concluding Thoughts

To meet policy mandates and professional standards for school, family, and community partnerships, school leaders must be aware of local issues facing their families and students and local resources to address those issues. Administrators therefore cannot limit their role to being school leaders but must also view themselves and act as community leaders. In Chapter 2, we discussed the school as an important community organization. Principals as school and community leaders must foster mutually beneficial and supportive relationships with others in the community. By providing space for community-based activities and events and participating in community functions, school administrators are better positioned to attract resources and goodwill toward the school and its mission; to broker goods and services for its students, faculty, staff, and families; and to contribute to the strength of the community and the social capital available to children and youth.

School administrators must also be aware of current research on partnerships, successful models of partnerships, and national trends and best practice on partnerships. Throughout this book, we have drawn from these research studies, models, and trends to describe why school, family, and community partnerships are critical to school improvement and excellence and how they can be implemented to be more inclusive of and responsive to all families, not just those traditionally involved.

Research and practice in the field, however, is continuously growing, and our knowledge base is expanding. By linking with national organizations, school leaders can find the resources they need to improve and refine their partnership efforts over time. Currently, there are several national organizations that provide support and information to educators and families on school, family, and community partnerships in K–12 settings. Among them are the following:

Coalition for Community Schools (CCS): CCS is an alliance of national, state, and local organizations in K–16 education, youth development, community planning and development, family support, health and human services, government and philanthropy, as well as national, state, and local community school networks. The coalition advocates for community schools as the vehicle for strengthening schools, families, and communities so that together they can improve student learning. For more information, visit www.communityschools.org.

Comer School Development Program: The Comer process, a school and systemwide intervention formulated by Dr. James P. Comer, Maurice Falk Professor of Child Psychiatry at the Yale University School of Medicine's Child Study Center, aims to bridge child psychiatry and education. The program is committed to the total development of all children by creating learning environments that support children's physical, cognitive, psychological, language, social, and ethical development. For more information, visit www.med.yale.edu.

Communities in Schools (CIS): CIS is the nation's largest dropout prevention organization. The mission of CIS is to connect needed community resources with schools to help young people successfully learn, stay in school, and prepare for life. By bringing caring adults into the schools to address children's unmet needs, CIS provides the link between educators and the community. For more information, visit www.cisnet.org.

Families and Schools Together (FAST): FAST is a nonprofit agency that designs and distributes family strengthening and parent involvement programs to help kids succeed in school and in life. The programs help families improve parenting skills and connect families to their schools. FAST brings together local support resources to build protective factors around kids and is dedicated to helping parents safeguard their families and prepare their children for success. For more information, visit www.familiesandschools.org.

Family Involvement Network of Educators (FINE): FINE is a national network of over 8,000 people interested in promoting strong partnerships among children's educators, their families, and their communities. FINE's membership is composed of faculty in higher education, school professionals, directors and trainers of community-based and national organizations, parent leaders, and graduate students. FINE was launched in November 2000 by Harvard Family Research Project (www.hfrp.org) to serve as a hub of resources for family engagement in children's education and to enable colleagues in the field to connect and communicate. FINE believes that engaging families and communities in education is essential to achieve high-performing schools and successful students. For more information, visit www.hfrp.org/family-involvement/fine-family-involvement-network-of-educators.

National Network of Partnership Schools (NNPS): Established at Johns Hopkins University in 1996, NNPS invites schools, districts, states, and organizations to join together and use research-based approaches to organize and sustain excellent programs of family and community involvement that will increase student success in school. "Based on more than two decades of research on parental involvement, family engagement, and community partnerships, NNPS' tools, guidelines, and action team approach may be used by all elementary, middle, and high schools to increase involvement and improve student learning and development," explains Dr. Joyce L. Epstein, founder and director of NNPS. NNPS also guides district leaders in helping their schools develop goal-oriented programs of family involvement and community connections and to meet NCLB requirements for parent involvement. In addition, NNPS assists state departments of education and organizations develop policies and take actions to support districts and schools in strengthening their partnership programs. For more information, visit www. partnershipschools.org.

National Parent Teacher Association (NPTA): As the largest volunteer child advocacy association in the nation, NPTA reminds the country of its obligations to children and provides parents and families with a powerful voice to speak on behalf of every child, while providing the best tools for parents to help their children be successful students. NPTA does not act alone. Working in cooperation with many national education, health, safety, and child advocacy groups and federal agencies, NPTA collaborates on projects that benefit children and that bring valuable resources to its members. For more information, visit www.pta.org.

In addition to national organizations, school leaders should contact district and state education leaders and their states' Parent Information and Resource Centers (PIRCs; www.pirc-info.net) to find out about local support for the implementation and evaluation of school, family, and community partnerships. By finding the most appropriate mix of national and local support, schools can ensure that they are kept abreast of research and promising practices for partnerships and thus best serve their families, communities, and students.

Finally, professional standards for school, family, and community partnerships highlight the importance of school leaders possessing professional dispositions that respect all families and communities, and understanding the role of school, family, and community partnerships in children and adolescents' development. In Chapters 3–6, we focused on four parent populations—fathers, families of children with disabilities, linguistically diverse families, and families living in poverty—whose needs are often overlooked in programs of school, family, and community partnerships. School leaders must bear in mind that, beyond these specific populations, many families in the United States are facing challenges that affect their capacity to parent effectively. These include job demands, conflicts or rivalries among children, children being overscheduled, and financial pressures. Moreover, these parents report a sense of "going it alone" in the vital task of raising their children and adolescents (SEARCH Institute, 2002). School leaders can ameliorate the isolation felt by many of these families by creating learning environments that assist them in supporting their children's well-being and school success.

In this book, we have strived to present information to help school leaders think about, develop, and evaluate inclusive partnership programs that promote the positive academic, social, and emotional development of *all* students. We know this work to be challenging. Some families and educators are more prepared for partnerships than others. Some districts and state departments of education are more supportive of partnerships than others. Some school leaders have more collaborative skills than others. However, we also know that the development of effective school, family, and community partnerships is possible and worthwhile; but it is a process that requires time. As partnerships develop over time, so do the professional, personal, and interpersonal skills of school leaders, teachers, and staff. In addition, families and communities develop greater respect and appreciation for educators and gain increased capacity to support children's learning. When school, family, and community partnerships are paired with excellent curricula and classroom instruction, the end result is stronger, more caring, and more responsive learning environments "for the children we share" (Epstein, 1995).

References

Adelman, H. S., & Taylor, L. (1998). Reframing mental health in schools and expanding school reform. *Educational Psychologist, 33,* 135–152.

Amato, P., & Rivera, F. (1999). Paternal involvement and children's behavior problems. *Journal of Marriage and the Family, 61,* 375–384.

Anastasiow, N. (1986). The research base for early intervention. *Journal of the Division for Early Childhood, 10*(2), 99–105.

Anderson, A. A. (2005). *The community builder's approach to theory of change: A practical guide to theory and development.* New York: The Aspen Institute Roundtable on Community Change.

Aparicio-Clark, A., & Dorris, A. (2006). Welcoming Latino parents as partners. *Principal Leadership, 7*(3), 22–25.

Astone, N., & McLanahan, S. (1991). Family structure, parental practices and high school completion. *American Sociological Review, 56,* 309–320.

Baker, A. J. L., Piotrkowski, C. S., & Brooks-Gunn, J. (1998). Effects of the Home Instruction Program for Preschool Youngsters (HIPPY) on children's school performance at the end of the program and one year later. *Early Childhood Research Quarterly, 13,* 571–588.

Baker, S., Gersten, R., & Keating, T. (2000). When less may be more: A 2-year longitudinal evaluation of a volunteer tutoring program requiring minimal training. *Reading Research Quarterly, 35,* 494–519.

Baker, S., Gersten, R., & Lee, D. (2002). A synthesis of empirical research on teaching mathematics to low-achieving students. *Elementary School Journal, 103,* 51–73.

Balli, S. J., Demo, D. H., & Wedman, J. F. (1998). Family involvement with children's homework: An intervention in the middle grades. *Family Relations, 47,* 149–157.

Belfield, C. R., & Levin, H. M. (2002). The effects of competition between schools on educational outcomes: A review for the United States. *Review of Educational Research, 72,* 279–341.

Bertrand, R., & Deslandes, R. (2005). Motivation of parent involvement in secondary-level schooling. *Journal of Educational Research, 98*(3), 164–175.

Beyers, J. M., Bates, J. E., Pettit, G. S., & Dodge, K. A. (2003). Neighborhood structure, parents' processes, and the development of youths' externalizing behaviors: A multi-level analysis. *American Journal of Community Psychology, 31,* 35–53.

Blank, M., Melaville, A., & Shah, B. (2003). *Making the difference: Research and practice in community schools.* Washington, DC: Coalition for Community Schools, Institute for Educational Leadership.

Bleeker, M. M., & Jacobs, J. E. (2004). Achievement in math and science: Do mothers' beliefs matter 12 years later? *Journal of Educational Psychology, 96,* 97–109.

Bomer, R., Dworin, J., May, L., & Semington, P. (2008). Miseducating teachers about the poor: A critical analysis of Ruby Paynes' claims about poverty. *Teachers College Record, 110*(12), 2497–2531.

Boothe, D. (2000). Looking beyond the ESL label. *Principal Leadership (Middle School Ed.), 1*(4), 30–35.

Bowen, N. K. (1999). A role for school social workers in promoting student success through school-family partnerships. *Social Work in Education, 21,* 34–47.

Bowen, N. K., & Bowen, G. L. (1999). Effects of crime and violence in neighborhoods and schools on the school behavior and performance of adolescents. *Journal of Adolescent Research, 14,* 319–342.

Bowen, N. K., Bowen, G. L., & Ware, W. B. (2002) Neighborhood social disorganization, families, and the educational behavior of adolescents. *Journal of Adolescent Research, 17,* 468–490.

Brewster, C., & Railsback, J. (2003). *Building trust with schools and diverse families: A foundation for lasting partnerships.* Portland, OR: Northwest Regional Educational Laboratory.

Bronfenbrenner, U. (1979). *The ecology of human development: Experiments by nature and design.* Cambridge, MA: Harvard University Press.

Bronfenbrenner, U. (1985). The three worlds of childhood. *Principal, 64,* 6–11.

Brownstein, J., Maushard, M., Robinson, J., Greenfeld, M., & Hutchins, D. (Eds.). (2006). *Promising partnership practices 2006.* Baltimore, MD: National Network of Partnership Schools. Retrieved August 20, 2008, at www.partnershipschools.org

Bryk, A. S., & Schneider, B. (2002). *Trust in schools: A core resource for improvement.* New York: Russell Sage Foundation.

Bryk, A. S., Sebring, P. B., Kerbow, D., Rollow, S., & Easton, J. Q. (1998). *Charting Chicago school reform: Democratic localism as a lever for Change.* Boulder, CO: Westview Press.

Burch, P., Palanki, A., & Davies, D. (1995*). From clients to partners: Four case studies of collaboration and family involvement in the development of school-linked services.* Report #29. Center on Families, Communities, Schools and Children's Learning. Baltimore: Johns Hopkins University.

Burello, L. C., & Wright, P. T. (Eds.). (1992). *Principal leadership. Principal letters: Practices for inclusive schools.* Bloomington: Indiana University, National Academy/CASE.

Cairney, T. H., & Rouge, J. (1997). *Community literacy practices and schooling: Towards effective support for students.* Sydney, Australia: Department of Employment, Education, Training and Youth Affairs.

Capps, R., Fix, M., Murray, J., Ost, J., Passel, J., & Herwantoro, S. (2005) *The new demography of America's schools: Immigration and the No Child Left Behind Act.* Washington, DC: The Urban Institute. Retrieved August 4, 2008, at http://www.urban.org/UploadedPDF/311230_new_demography.pdf

Caspe, M. (2001). *Family-school-community partnerships: A compilation of professional standards of practice.* Cambridge, MA: Harvard Family Research Project.

Cassity, J., & Harris, S. (2000). Parents of ESL students: A study of parental involvement. *NASSP Bulletin, 84*(619), 55–62.

Catsambis, S. (2001). Expanding knowledge of parental involvement in children's secondary education: Connections with high school seniors' academic success. *Social Psychology of Education, 5,* 149–177.

Center for Disease Control. (2002). Cohabitation, marriage, divorce, and remarriage in the United States. National Center for Health Statistics. *Vital Health Statistics, 23*(22).

Chaskin, R. J., & Rauner, D. M. (1995). Toward a field of caring: An epilogue. *Phi Delta Kappan, 76,* 718.

Chen, X. (2001). *Efforts by public K–8 schools to involve parents in children's education: Do school and parent reports agree?* Washington, DC: U.S. Department of Education, National Center for Education Statistics 2001–076.

Chrispeels, J. (1996). Effective schools and home-school-community partnership roles: A framework for parent involvement. *School Effectiveness and School Improvement, 7,* 297–322.

Chung, C. (2007). *The education of homeless children.* Paper presented at the annual meeting of the American Educational Research Association, Chicago, Illinois.

Cimmarusti, R. A., James, M. C., Simpson, D. W., & Wright, C. E. (1984). Treating the context of truancy. *Social Work in Education, 6,* 201–211.

Clark, R. (2002). Ten hypotheses about what predicts student achievement for African American students and all other students: What the research shows. In W. R. Allen, M. B. Spencer, & C. O'Conner (Eds.), *African American education: Race, community, inequality, and achievement: A tribute to Edgar G. Epps* (pp. 155–178). Oxford, UK: Elsevier Science.

Colina, S., & Sykes, J. (2004). Educating parents in the Spanish-speaking community: A look at translated educational materials. *Bilingual Research Journal, 28*(3), 299–318.

Comer, J. (1993). *School power: Implications of an intervention project.* New York: Free Press.

Comer, J., & Haynes, M. (1991). Parent involvement in schools: An ecological approach. *Elementary School Journal, 91,* 271–278.

Congress of the United States of America. (1975). Public Law 94-142, Education for All Handicapped Children Act. In E. Provenzo (Ed.), *Critical issues in education: An anthology of readings.* Thousand Oaks, CA: Sage.

Corville-Smith, J., Ryan, B. A., Adams, G. R., & Dalicandro, T. (1998). Distinguishing absentee students from regular attenders: The combined influence of personal, family, and school factors. *Journal of Youth and Adolescence, 27,* 629–649.

Council of Chief State School Officers (CCSSO). (2008). Educational Leadership Policy Standards: ISLLC 2008, as adopted by the National Policy Board for Educational Administration. Retrieved on January 11, 2008, at http://www.ccsso.org

Critchfield, A. J., Axelrod, R., Debebe, G., Davis, E. B., Offermann, L. R., & Costanza, D. P. (2004, November). *Culture-bound or culture-free? Multidisciplinary perspectives on leadership in organizations.* Symposium conducted at the annual meeting of the International Leadership Association, Washington, DC.

Crowter, K., & South, S. (2003). Neighborhood distress and school dropout: The variable significance of community context. *Social Science Research, 32*(4), 659–698.

Dauber, S. L., & Epstein, J. L. (1993). Parents' attitudes and practices of involvement in inner-city elementary and middle schools. In N. Chavkin (Ed.), *Families and schools in a pluralistic society* (pp. 53–71). Albany, NY: SUNY Press.

Davalos, D. B., Chavez, E. L., & Guardiola, R. J. (2005). Effects of perceived parental school support and family communication on delinquent behaviors in Latino and white non-Latinos. *Cultural Diversity and Ethnic Minority Psychology, 11,* 57–68.

Davis-Kean, P., & Eccles, J. (2005). Influences and challenges to better parent-school collaborations. In E. Patrikakou, R. Weissberg, S. Redding, & H. Walberg (Eds.), *School-family partnerships for children's success* (pp. 57–76). New York: Teachers College Press.

Decker, L., Decker, V., & Brown, P. (2007). *Diverse partnerships for student success: Strategies and tools to help school leaders.* Lanham, MD: Rowman & Littlefield Education.

Desimone, L. (1999). Linking parent involvement with student achievement: Do race and income matter? *The Journal of Educational Research, 93,* 11–30.

Desimone, L., Finn-Stevenson, M., & Henrich, C. (2000). Whole school reform in a low-income African American community: The effects of the CoZi model on teachers, parents, and students. *Urban Education, 35,* 269–323.

DiCerbo, P. (2000). Common practices for uncommon learners: Addressing linguistic and cultural diversity. In *Framing effective practice: Topics and issues in education English language learners* (pp. 3–12). Washington, DC: Institute for Education Policy Studies, George Washington University. Retrieved August 4, 2008, at www.ncela.gwu.edu

Domina, T. (2005). Leveling the home advantage: Assessing the effectiveness of parental involvement in elementary school. *Sociology of Education, 78,* 233–249.

Donahue, P. L., Finnegan, R. J., Lutkus, A. D., Allen, N. L., & Campbell, J. R. (2001). *The nation's report card: Fourth-grade reading 2002.* NCES 2001-499. Washington, DC: U.S. Department of Education, Office of Educational Research and Improvement, National Center for Education Statistics.

Dryfoos, J., & Maguire, S. (2002). *Inside full-service community schools.* Thousand Oaks, CA: Corwin.

Duckworth, K., & DeJung, J. (1989). Inhibiting class cutting among high school students. *The High School Journal, 72,* 188–195.

Eccles, J. E., Adler, T., & Kaczala, C. M. (1982). Socialization of achievement attitudes and beliefs: Parental influences. *Child Development, 53,* 310–321.

Eccles, J. S., & Harold, R. D. (1993). Parent-school involvement during the early adolescent years. *Teachers College Record, 94*(3), 568–587.

Eccles, J. S., & Harold, R. D. (1996). Family involvement in children's and adolescents' schooling. In A. Bloom & J. F. Dunn (Eds.), *Family-school links: How do they affect educational outcomes?* (pp. 3–34). Mahwah, NJ: Erlbaum.

Edwards, P. A., Pleasants, H. M., & Franklin, S. H. (1999). *A path to follow: Learning to listen to parents.* Portsmouth, NH: Heinemann.

Elliott, D. S., Wilson, W. J., Huizinga, D., Sampson, R. J., Elliott, A., & Rankin, B. (1996). The effects of neighborhood disadvantage on adolescent development. *Journal of Research in Crime and Delinquency, 33,* 389–426.

Epstein, J. L. (1986). Parents' reactions to teacher practices of parent involvement. *Elementary School Journal, 79,* 277–294.

Epstein, J. L. (1991). Effects on student achievement of teacher practices of parent involvement. In S. Silvern (Ed.), *Advances in reading/language research: Literacy through family, community, and school interaction* (Vol. 5; pp. 261–276). Greenwich, CT: JAI.

Epstein, J. L. (1995, May). School/family/community partnerships: Caring for the children we share. *Phi Delta Kappan, 76,* 701–712.

Epstein, J. L. (2001). *School, family, and community partnerships: Preparing educators and improving schools.* Boulder, CO: Westview.

Epstein, J. L., & Dauber, S. L. (1991). School programs and teacher practices of parent involvement in inner-city elementary and middle schools. *Elementary School Journal, 91,* 289–305.

Epstein, J. L., & Sanders, M. G. (2006). Prospects for change: Preparing educators for school, family, and community partnerships. *Peabody Journal of Education, 81,* 81–120.

Epstein, J. L., Sanders, M. G., Simon, B. S., Salinas, K. C., Jansorn, N. R., & Van Voorhis, F. L. (2002). *School, family, and community partnerships: Your handbook for action* (2nd ed.). Thousand Oaks, CA: Corwin.

Epstein, J. L., & Sheldon, S. B. (2002). Present and accounted for: Improving student attendance through family and community involvement. *Journal of Educational Research, 95,* 308–318.

Epstein, J. L., Simon, B. S., & Salinas, K. C. (1997, September). Effects of Teachers Involve Parents in Schoolwork (TIPS) language arts interactive homework in the middle grades. *Research Bulletin, 18.* Bloomington, IN: Phi Delta Kappa, CEDR.

Faires, J., Nichols, W. D., & Rickelman, R. J. (2000). Effects of parental involvement in developing competent readers in first grade. *Reading Psychology, 21,* 195–215.

Falbo, T., Lein, L., & Amador, N. A. (2001). Parental involvement during the transition to high school. *Journal of Adolescent Research, 16,* 511–529.

Fass, S., & Cauther, N. (2007). *Who are America's poor children?* National Center for Children in Poverty (NCCP). Retrieved August 31, 2008, at www.nccp.org

Fine, M. (1993). (Ap)Parent involvement: Reflections on parents, power, and urban public schools. *Teachers College Record, 94,* 682–710.

Fitzgerald, J. (2001). Can minimally trained college student volunteers help young at-risk students to read better? *Reading Research Quarterly, 36,* 28–46.

Flouri, E., & Buchanan, A. (2004). Early father's and mother's involvement and child's later educational outcomes. *British Journal of Educational Psychology, 74,* 141–153.

Frome, P. M., & Eccles, J. S. (1998). Parents' influence on children's achievement-related perceptions. *Journal of Personality and Social Psychology, 74,* 435–452.

Fu, D. (2004). Teaching ELL students in regular classrooms at the secondary level. *Voices from the Middle, 11*(4),8–15.

Fullan, M. (2001). *Leading in a culture of change.* San Francisco, CA: Jossey-Bass.

Furstenberg, F., Jr., Cook, T., Eccles, J., Elder, G., Jr., & Sameroff, A. (2000). *Managing to make it: Urban families and adolescent success.* Chicago: University of Chicago Press.

Gal, I., & Stoudt, A. (1995, September). *Family achievement in mathematics.* NCAL Connections. National Center on Adult Literacy, University of Pennsylvania, Philadelphia.

Gamse, B., Millsap, M., & Goodson, B. (2002). When implementation threatens impact: Challenging lessons from evaluating educational programs. *Peabody Journal of Education, 77*(4), 146–166.

George, R., & Kaplan, D. (1998). A structural model of parent and teacher influences on science attitudes of eighth graders: Evidence of NELS:88. *Science Education, 82,* 93–109.

Goddard, R. D., Sweetland, S. R., & Hoy, W. K. (2000). Academic emphasis of urban elementary schools and student achievement in reading and mathematics: A multilevel analysis. *Educational Administration Quarterly, 36,* 683–702.

Goldhaber, D. D., & Eide, E. R. (2002). What do we know (and need to know) about the impact of school choice reforms on disadvantaged students? *Harvard Educational Review, 72,* 157–176.

Gonzales-DeHass, A. R., Willems, P. P., & Holbein, M. F. D. (2005). Examining the relationship between parental involvement and student motivation. *Educational Psychology Review, 17,* 99–123.

Gorksi, P. (2005). *Savage unrealities: Uncovering classism in Ruby Payne's framework* (abridged version). Retrieved January 12, 2009, at http://www.edchange.org/publications/Savage_Unrealities_abridged.pdf

Gottfredson, D. C., Gottfredson, G. D., & Hybl, L. G. (1993). Managing adolescent behavior: A multiyear, multischool study. *American Educational Research Journal, 30*(1), 179–215.

Gottfredson, G. D., Gottfredson, D. C., Payne, A. A., & Gottfredson, N. C. (2005). School climate predictors of school disorder: Results from a national study of delinquency prevention in schools. *Journal of Research in Crime and Delinquency, 42,* 412–444.

Gray, B. (1991). *Collaborating: Finding common ground for multiparty problems.* San Francisco: Jossey-Bass.

Greenleaf, C. L., Schoenbach, R., Cziko, C., & Mueller, F. L. (2001). Apprenticing adolescent readers to academic literacy. *Harvard Educational Review, 71,* 79–129.

Griffith, J. (1998). The relation of school structure and social environment to parent involvement in elementary schools. *Elementary School Journal, 99,* 53–80.

Grolnick, W. S., Kurowski, C. O., Dunlap, K. G., & Hevey, C. (2000). Parental resources and the transition to junior high. *Journal of Research on Adolescence, 10,* 465–488.

Gutman, L. M., & Midgley, C. (2000). The role of protective factors in supporting the academic achievement of poor African American students during the middle school transition. *Journal of Youth and Adolescence, 29,* 223–248.

Halford, J. (1996). How parent liaisons connect families to school. *Educational Leadership, 53*(7), 4–36.

Hallinger, P., & Heck, R. (1998). Exploring the principal's contribution to school effectiveness: 1980–1995. *School Effectiveness and School Improvement, 9,* 157–191.

Halsey, P. (2005). Parent involvement in junior high schools: A failure to communicate. *American Secondary Education, 34*(1), 57–69.

Harris, E. (2005). Ask the expert: An introduction to theory of change. *The Evaluation Exchange, 11*(2), 12 & 19.

Harry, B., Allen, N., & McLaughlin, M. (1995). Communication versus compliance: African American parents' involvement in special education. *Exceptional Children, 61,* 364–377.

Harry, B., Klinger, J., & Hart, J. (2005). African American families under fire. *Remedial and Special Education, 26*(2), 101–112.

Haynes, N. M., Comer, J. P., & Hamilton-Lee, M. (1989). School climate enhancement through parental involvement. *Journal of School Psychology, 27,* 87–90.

Heath, S. B. (1983). *Ways with words.* New York: Cambridge University Press.

Heath, S. B., & McLaughlin, M. (1996). The best of both worlds: Connecting schools and community youth organizations for all-day all-year learning. In J. Cibulka and W. Kritek (Eds.), *Coordination among schools, families, and communities* (pp. 50–68). Buffalo: State University of New York Press.

Heibert, E. H. (1980). The relationship of logical reasoning ability, oral language comprehension, and home experiences to preschool children's print awareness. *Journal of Reading Behavior, 12,* 313–324.

Helm, C. M., & Burkett, C. W. (1989). Effects of computer-assisted telecommunications on school attendance. *Journal of Educational Research, 82,* 362–365.

Henderson, A., & Mapp, K. L. (2002). *A new wave of evidence: The impact of school, family, and community connections on student achievement.* Austin, TX: Southwest Educational Development Laboratory.

Henderson, A., Mapp, K., Johnson, V., & Davies, D. (2007). *Beyond the bake sale: The essential guide to family-school partnerships.* New York: New Press.

Hernandez, D. J., & Brandon, P. D. (2002). Who are the fathers of today? In C. Tamis-LeMonda & N. Cabrera (Eds.), *Handbook of father involvement: Multidisciplinary perspectives* (pp. 33–62). Mahwah, NJ: Erlbaum.

Hill, N. E., Castellino, D. R., Lansford, J. E., Nowlin, P., Dodge, K. A., Bates, J. E., & Pettit, G. S. (2004). Parent academic involvement as related to school behavior, achievement, and aspirations: Demographic variations across adolescence. *Child Development, 75,* 1491–1509.

Ho, E. S., & Willms, J. D. (1996). Effects of parental involvement on eighth-grade achievement, *Sociology of Education, 69,* 126–141.

Hofferth, S. L., Pleck, J., Stueve, J. L., Bianchi, S., & Sayer, L. (2002). The demography of fathers: What fathers do. In C. Tamis-LeMonda & N. Cabrera (Eds.), *Handbook of father involvement: Multidisciplinary perspectives* (pp. 63–90). Mahwah, NJ: Erlbaum.

Hoffman, J. V. (1991). Teacher and school effects in learning to read. In R. Barr, M. L. Kamil, P. B. Mosenthal, & P. D. Pearson (Eds.), *Handbook of reading research* (Vol. 2; pp. 911–950). New York: Longman.

Hong, S., & Ho, H. (2005). Direct and Indirect longitudinal effects of parental involvement on student achievement: Second-order latent growth modeling across ethnic groups. *Journal of Educational Psychology, 97,* 32–42.

Hoover-Dempsey, K. V., Walker, J., & Sandler, H. M. (2005). Parents' motivation for involvement in their children's education. In E. Patrikakou, R. Weissberg, S. Redding, & H. Walberg (Eds.), *School-family partnerships for children's success* (pp. 40–56). New York: Teachers College Press.

Horvat, E., Weininger, E., & Lareau, A. (2003). From social ties to social capital: Class differences in the relation between school and parent networks. *American Educational Research Journal, 40*(2), 319–351.

Howland, A., Anderson, J., Smiley, A., & Abbott, D. (2006). School liaisons: Bridging the gap between home and school. *The School Community Journal, 16*(2), 47–68.

Hutchins, D., Maushard, M., O'Donnell, C., Greenfeld, M., & Thomas, B. (Eds.). (2008). *Promising partnership practices 2008.* Baltimore, MD: National Network of Partnership Schools. Retrieved August 20, 2008, at www.partnershipschools.org

Hyde, J. S., Else-Quest, N. M., Alibali, M. W., Knuth, E., & Romberg, T. (2006). Mathematics in the home: Homework practices and mother-child interactions doing mathematics. *Journal of Mathematical Behavior, 25,* 136–152.

Jacobs, J. (1991). Influence of gender stereotypes on parent and child mathematics attitudes. *Journal of Educational Psychology, 83,* 518–527.

Jeynes, W. (2003). A meta-analysis: The Effects of parental involvement on minority children's academic achievement. *Education and Urban Society, 35*(2), 202–218.

Johnson, B., Jr. (1998). Organizing for collaboration: A reconsideration of some basic organizing principles. In D. Pounder (Ed.), *Restructuring schools for collaboration: Promises and pitfalls* (pp. 9–26). Albany: State University of New York Press.

Johnson, B., Jr., & Ginsberg, M. (1996, November). Building capacity through school support teams. *Educational Leadership, 54,* 80–82.

Jordan, C., Orozco, E., & Averett, A. (2001). *Emerging issues in school, family, and community connections.* Austin, TX: Southwest Educational Development Laboratory.

Jordan, G. E., Snow, C. E., & Porche, M. V. (2000). Project EASE: The effect of a family literacy project on kindergarten students' early literacy skills. *Reading Research Quarterly, 35,* 524–546.

Keith, T. Z. (1991). Parental involvement and achievement in high school. *Advances in reading/language research: Literacy through family, community, and school interaction* (Vol. 5, pp. 125–141). Greenwich, CT: JAI Press.

Keith, T. Z., Keith, P. B., Quirk, K. J., Sperduto, J., Santillo, S., & Killings, S. (1998). Longitudinal effects of parent involvement on high school grades: Similarities and differences across gender and ethnic groups. *Journal of School Psychology, 36,* 335–363.

Kellogg Foundation. (1998). *W. K. Kellogg Foundation evaluation handbook.* Battle Creek, MI: Kellogg Foudation.

King, V. (1994). Nonresident father involvement and child well-being: Can dads make a difference? *Journal of Family Issues, 15,* 78–96.

Kirschenbaum, H. (1999). Night and day: Succeeding with parents at school. *Principal, 78*(3), 20–23.

Koball, H., Douglas-Hall, A., & Chau, M. (2005). *Children in urban areas are increasingly low income.* New York: National Center for Children in Poverty. Retrieved on September 21, 2007, at http://nccp.org/publications/pub_637.html

Lake, J., & Billingsley, B. (2000). An analysis of factors that contribute to parent-school conflict in special education. *Remedial and Special Education, 21*(4), 240–251.

Lareau, A. (2000). Social class and the daily lives of children: A study from the United States. *Childhood: A Global Journal of Child Research, 7,* 155–171.

Lawrence-Lightfoot, S. (1978). *Worlds apart: Relationships between families and schools.* New York: Basic Books.

Lawrence-Lightfoot, S. (2003). *The essential conversation: What parents and teachers can learn from each other.* New York: Random House.

League, S.E., & Ford, L. (1996, March). *Fathers' involvement in their children's special education program.* Paper presented at the annual meeting of the National Association of School Psychologists, Atlanta, Georgia. (ERIC Document Reproduction Service No. ED400632)

Lee, V. E., & Croninger, R. G. (1994). The relative importance of home and school in development of literacy skills for middle-grade students. *American Journal of Education, 102,* 286–329.

Leichter, H. J. (1984). Families as environments for literacy. In H. Goelman, A. Oberg, & F. Smith (Eds.), *Awakening to literacy* (pp. 38–50). London: Heinemann Educational Books.

Leithwood, K. (1994). Leadership for school restructuring. *Educational Administration Quarterly, 30*(4), 498–518.

Lerner, R., & Shumow, L. (1997). Aligning the construction zones of parents and teachers for mathematics reform. *Cognition and Instruction, 15,* 41–83.

Leslie, L., & Allen, L. (1999). Factors that predict success in an early literacy intervention project. *Reading Research Quarterly, 34,* 404–424.

Lewis, A. (2000). Middle grades liaisons do "whatever it takes" to reach out and bring in parents. *Reforming Middle Schools & School Systems, 4*(1), 1–4.

Licht, B. G., Gard, T., & Guardino, C. (1991). Modifying school attendance of special education high school students. *Journal of Educational Research, 84,* 368–373.

Lindeman, B. (2002). Speaking their language: Successfully reaching out to immigrant parents just requires a few simple steps. *Instructor, 112*(2), 34–36.

Linn, R. L., & Haug, C. (2002). Stability of school-building accountability scores and gains. *Educational Evaluation and Policy Analysis, 24,* 29–36.

Lipsitz, J. (1995). Prologue: Why we should care about caring. *Phi Delta Kappan, 76,* 665–666.

Lonigan, C. J., & Whitehurst, G. J. (1998). Relative efficacy of parent and teacher involvement in a shared-reading intervention for preschool children from low-income backgrounds. *Early Childhood Research Quarterly, 13,* 263–290.

Loprest, P., & Acs, G. (1996). *Profile of disability among families on AFDC.* Washington, DC: Urban Institute.

Lortie, D. (2002). *Schoolteacher: A sociological study.* Chicago: University of Chicago Press.

Ma, X. (1999). Dropping out of advanced mathematics: The effects of parental involvement. *Teachers College Record, 101,* 60–81.

Ma, X. (2001). Bullying and being bullied: To what extent are bullies also victims? *American Educational Research Journal, 38*, 351–370.

Mapp, K. L. (2002). Having their say: Parents describe why and how they are engaged in their children's learning. *School Community Journal, 13*, 35–64.

Marchant, G. J., Paulson, S. E., & Rothlisberg, B. A. (2001). Relations of middle school students' perceptions of family and school contexts with academic achievement. *Psychology in the Schools, 38*, 505–519.

Marks, H. M., & Printy, S. M. (2003). Principal leadership and school performance: An integration of transformational and instructional leadership. *Educational Administration Quarterly, 39*, 370–397.

Marsiglio, W., Amato, P., Day, R. D., & Lamb, M. E. (2000). Scholarship on fatherhood in the 1990s and beyond. *Journal of Marriage and the Family, 62*, 1173–1191.

Mathematica Policy Research Inc. & Center for Children and Families at Teachers College, Columbia University. (2001). *Building their futures: How early head start programs are changing the lives of infants and toddlers in low-income families.* Washington, DC: Administration on Children, Youth, and Families, Department of Health and Human Services. Retrieved from www.acf.dhhs.gov (research reports).

Maushard, M., Martin, C., Hutchins, D., Greenfeld, M., Thomas, B., Fournier, A., & Pickett, G. (Eds.). (2007). *Promising partnership practices 2007.* Baltimore, MD: National Network of Partnership Schools. Retrieved August 20, 2008, at www.partnershipschools.org

McBride, B. A., & Rane, T. R. (1996). Father/male involvement in early childhood programs. *Human Development and Family Life Bulletin, 2*(3). Retrieved September 20, 2007, at www.hec.ohio-state.edu/famlife/bulletin/volume.2/bull23p.htm

McBride, B. A., & Rane, T. R. (1997). Father/male involvement in early childhood programs: Issues and challenges. *Early Childhood Education Journal, 25*, 11–15.

McCarthey, S. (1999). Identifying teacher practices that connect home and school. *Education and Urban Society, 32*, 83–107.

McDermott, D. (2008). *Developing caring relationships among parents, children, school, and communities.* Thousand Oaks, CA: Sage.

McNeal, R. B. (1999). Parental involvement as social capital: Differential effectiveness on science achievement, truancy, and dropping out. *Social Forces, 78*, 117–144.

McPartland, J. M., & Nettles, S. M. (1991). Using community adults as advocates or mentors for at-risk middle school students: A two-year evaluation of project RAISE. *American Journal of Education, 99*, 568–586.

Menning, C. (2006). Nonresident fathering and school failure. *Journal of Family Issues, 27*, 1356–1382.

MetLife. (2005). *The MetLife Survey of the American Teacher, 2004–2005, transitions and the role of supportive relationships.* New York: MetLife.

Meyer, J., & Mann, M. (2006). Teachers' perception of the benefits of home visits for early elementary children. *Early Childhood Education Journal, 34*(1), 93–97.

Miles-Bonart, S. (2002). A look at variables affecting parent satisfaction with IEP meetings. In *No Child Left Behind: The vital role of rural schools.* 22nd Annual National Conference Proceedings of the American Council on Rural Special Education, March 7–9, 2002, Reno, Nevada. (ERIC Document Reproduction Service No. ED463119)

Misra, S. (2006). *SLIIDEA: Increasing involvement of parents of children with disabilities.* Retrieved February 2007 at www.projectforum.org

Moles, O. (1996). *Reaching all families: Creating family-friendly schools.* Washington, DC: Office of Educational Research and Improvement, U.S. Department of Education. Report ED400117.

Moles, O. (2005). School-family relations and student learning: Federal education initiatives. In E. Patrikakou, R. Weissberg, S. Redding, & H. Walberg (Eds.), *School-family partnerships for children's success* (pp. 131–147). New York: Teachers College Press.

Munn-Joseph, M., & Gavin-Evans, K. (2008). Urban parents of children with special needs: Advocating for their children through social networks. *Urban Education, 43*, 378–393.

Muraskin, L. D. (1993). *Understanding evaluation: The way to better prevention programs*. Washington, DC: U.S. Department of Education.

National Association for the Education of Young Children (NAEYC). (2008). *Critical facts about young children and early childhood programs in the United States*. Washington, DC: Author. Retrieved April, 28, 2008, at www.naeyc.org/ece/critical/facts1.asp

National Center for Children in Poverty (NCCP). (n.d.). *Child poverty and family economic hardship: 10 important questions*. Retrieved August 4, 2008, at www.nccp.org

National Center for Education Statistics. (1997). *Job satisfaction among America's teachers: Effects of workplace conditions, background characteristics, and teacher compensation*. Retrieved October 15, 2007, at http://nces.ed.gov/pubs97/web/97471

National Center for Fathering. (2008). *Father's involvement in children's learning: Comparisons 2008 vs. 1999*. Retrieved January 6, 2009, at http://www.fathers.com/research

National Center on Family Homelessness. (1999). *Homeless children: America's new outcasts*. Newton Centre, MA: Author.

National Coalition for Parent Involvement in Education (NCPIE). (2004). *NCLB action briefs: Parental involvement*. Retrieved December 5, 2008, at http://www.ncpie.org/nclbaction/parent_involvement.html

National Research Council. (2003). *Engaging schools: Fostering high school students' motivation to learn*. Washington, DC: National Academies Press.

Neild, R. C. (2005). Parent management of school choice in a large urban district. *Urban Education, 40*, 270–297.

Nettles, S. M. (1991). Community contributions to school outcomes of African-American students. *Education and Urban Society, 24*, 132–147.

Newman, K., & Chen, V. (2007). *The missing class: Portraits of the near poor in America*. Boston, MA: Beacon Press.

Newman, L. (2005). *Parents' satisfaction with their children's schooling*. Washington, DC: U.S. Office of Special Education Programs.

Niemiec, R., Sikorski, M., & Walberg, H. (1999). Designing school volunteer programs. *NASSP Bulletin, 83*, 114–116.

Noddings, N. (1995). Teaching themes of care. *Phi Delta Kappan, 76*(3), 675–679.

Noguera, P. A. (1995). Preventing and producing violence: A critical analysis of responses to school violence. *Harvard Educational Review, 65*, 189–212.

Noguera, P. A. (1999, May). Transforming urban schools through investments in the social capital of parents. *Motion Magazine*. Retrieved at http://www.inmotionmagazine.com

Offermann, L. R., & Phan, L. U. (2002). Culturally intelligent leadership for a diverse world. In R. E. Riggio, S. E. Murphy, & F. J. Pirozzolo (Eds.), *Multiple intelligences and leadership* (pp. 187–214). Mahwah, NJ: Lawrence Erlbaum Associates.

Ogawa, R., & Bossert, S. (1995). Leadership as an organizational quality. *Educational Administration Quarterly, 31*, 224–243.

Paratore, J. R., Hindin, A., Krol-Sinclair, B., & Duran, P. (1999). Discourse between teachers and Latino parents during conferences based on home literacy portfolios. *Education and Urban Society, 32*, 58–82.

Parcel, T. L., & Dufur, M. J. (2001). Capital at home and at school: Effects on students' achievement. *Social Forces, 79*, 881–912.

Parke, R. D., McDowell, D. J., Kim, M., Killian, C., Dennis, J., Flyr, M. L., & Wild, M. N. (2002). Fathers' contribution to children's peer relationships. In C. Tamis-LeMonda & N. Cabrera (Eds.), *Handbook of father involvement: Multidisciplinary perspectives* (pp. 141–168). Mahwah, NJ: Erlbaum.

Parsons, J. E., Adler, T., & Kaczala, C. M. (1982). Socialization of achievement attitudes and beliefs: Parental influences. *Child Development, 53*, 310–321.

Phillips, L. M., Norris, S. P., & Mason, J. M. (1996). Longitudinal effects of early literacy concepts on reading achievement: A kindergarten intervention and five-year follow-up. *Journal of Literacy Research, 28*, 173–195.

Purcell-Gates, V. (1996). Stories, coupons, and the TV guide: Relationships between home literacy experiences and emergent literacy knowledge. *Reading Research Quarterly, 31,* 406–428.

Purkey, S. C., & Smith, M. S. (1983). Effective schools: A review. *The Elementary School Journal, 83,* 426–452.

Purkey, S. C., & Smith, M. S. (1985). School reform: The district policy implications of the effective schools literature. *Elementary School Journal, 85*(3), 353–389.

Reisner, E. R. (2004). *Using evaluation methods to promote continuous improvement and accountability in after-school programs: A guide.* Washington, DC: Policy Studies Associates.

Reynolds, A. J., & Walberg, H. J. (1992). A structural model of science achievement and attitude: An extension to high school. *Journal of Educational Psychology, 84,* 371–382.

Roderick, M., Arney, M., Axelman, M., DaCosta, K., Steiger, C., Stone, S., Villearreal-Sosa, L., & Waxman, E. (1997). *Habits hard to break: A new look at truancy in Chicago's public high schools.* Chicago: School of Social Service Administration, University of Chicago.

Roman, C., & Moore, G. (2004). *Measuring local institutions and organizations: The role of community institutional capacity in social capital.* Washington, DC: Urban Institute.

Rosenberg, M., Westling, D., & McLeskey, J. (2008). *Special education for today's teachers.* Upper Saddle River, NJ: Prentice Hall.

Rosenholz, S. J. (1989). *Teachers' workplace: The social organization of schools.* White Plains, NY: Longman.

Salas, L. (2004). Voices: Community, parents, teachers, and students: Individualized Educational Plan (IEP) meetings and Mexican American parents: Let's talk about it. *Journal of Latinos and Education, 3*(3), 181–192.

Salinas, K., & Rodriguez-Jansorn, N., with Neuman, B., & Harvey, A. (2003). *Promising partnership practices 2003.* Baltimore, MD: National Network of Partnership Schools. Retrieved August 20, 2008, at www.partnershipschools.org

Sanders, M. G. (1996). School-family-community partnerships focused on school safety. *Journal of Negro Education, 65*(3), 369–374.

Sanders, M. G. (1998). The effects of school, family, and community support on the academic achievement of African American adolescents. *Urban Education, 33,* 385–409.

Sanders, M. G. (2000). Creating successful school-based partnership programs with families of special needs students. *The School Community Journal, 10*(2), 37–56.

Sanders, M. G. (2001). The role of "community" in comprehensive school, family, and community partnership programs. *Elementary School Journal, 102,* 19–34.

Sanders, M. G. (2005). *Building school-community partnerships: Collaboration for student success.* Thousand Oaks, CA: Corwin.

Sanders, M. G. (2008). How parent liaisons can help bridge home and school. *Journal of Educational Research, 101*(5), 287–297.

Sanders, M. G., & Epstein, J. L. (2000a). Building school-family-community partnerships in middle and high schools. In M. G. Sanders (Ed.), *Schooling students placed at risk* (pp. 339–362). Mahwah, NJ: Erlbaum.

Sanders, M. G., & Epstein, J. L. (2000b). The National Network of Partnership Schools: How research influences educational practice. *Journal of Education for Students Placed at Risk, 5*(1&2), 61–76.

Sanders, M. G., & Harvey, A. (2002). Beyond the school walls: A case study of principal leadership for school-community collaboration. *Teachers College Record, 104*(7), 1345–1368.

Sanders, M. G., & Herting, J. R. (2000). Gender and the effects of school, family, and church support on the academic achievement of African-American urban adolescents. In M. G. Sanders (Ed.), *Schooling students placed at risk: Research, policy, and practice in the education of poor and minority adolescents* (pp. 141–161). Mahwah, NJ: Lawrence Erlbaum Associates.

Sanders, M. G., & Lewis, K. (2004). Partnerships at an urban high school: Meeting the parent involvement requirements of No Child Left Behind. *E-Journal of Teaching and Learning in Diverse Settings, 2*(1), 1–21.

Sanders, M. G., & Simon, B. S. (2002). A comparison of program development at elementary, middle, and high schools in the National Network of Partnership Schools. *The School Community Journal, 12*(1), 7–27.

Scarborough, H. S., & Dobrich, W. (1994). On the efficacy of reading to preschoolers. *Developmental Review, 14,* 245–302.

Schulting, A. B., Malone, P. S., & Dodge, K. A. (2005). The effect of school-based kindergarten transition policies and practices on child academic outcomes. *Developmental Psychology, 41,* 840–871.

SEARCH Institute. (2002). *Building strong families.* Minneapolis, MN: Author. Retrieved February 2007 at www.search-institute.org

Seltzer, J. A. (1994). Consequences of marital dissolution for children. *Annual Review of Sociology, 20,* 235–266.

Sénéchal, M., & LeFevre, J. (2002). Parental involvement in the development of children's reading skill: A five-year longitudinal study. *Child Development, 73,* 455–460.

Sénéchal, M., LeFevre, J., Thomas, E., & Daley, K. (1998). Differential effects of home literacy experiences on the development of oral and written language. *Reading Research Quarterly, 32,* 96–116.

Shaver, A. V., & Walls, R. T. (1998). Effect of Title I parent involvement on student reading and math achievement. *Journal of Research and Development in Education, 321,* 90–97.

Sheldon, S. B. (2002). Parents' social networks and beliefs as predictors of parent involvement. *Elementary School Journal, 102*(4), 301–316.

Sheldon, S. B. (2005). Testing a structural equations model of partnership program implementation and family involvement. *Elementary School Journal, 106,* 171–187.

Sheldon, S. B. (2007). Improving student attendance with school, family, and community partnerships. *Journal of Educational Research, 100,* 267–275.

Sheldon, S. B., & Epstein, J. L. (2002). Improving student behavior and school discipline with family and community involvement. *Education and Urban Society, 35,* 4–26.

Sheldon, S. B., & Epstein, J. L. (2005). School programs of family and community involvement to support children's reading and literacy development across the grades. In J. Flood & P. Anders (Eds.), *Literacy development of students in urban schools: Research and policy* (pp. 107–138). Newark, DE: International Reading Association (IRA).

Sheldon, S. B., Epstein, J. L., & Galindo, C. L. (in press). Not just numbers: Creating a partnership climate to improve students' math proficiency. *School Leadership and Policy Studies.*

Sheldon, S. B., & Van Voorhis, F. L. (2004). Partnership programs in U.S. schools: Their development and relationship to family involvement outcomes. *School Effectiveness and School Improvement, 15*(2), 125–148.

Shumow, L., & Miller, J. D. (2001). Parents' at-home and at-school academic involvement with young adolescents. *Journal of Early Adolescence, 21,* 68–91.

Simon, B. S. (2001). Family involvement in high school: Predictors and effects. *NASSP Bulletin, 85,* 8–19.

Simon, B. S. (2004). High school outreach and family involvement. *Social Psychology of Education, 7,* 185–209.

Simons-Morton, B. G., & Crump, A. D. (2003). Association of parental involvement and social competence with school adjustment and engagement among sixth graders. *Journal of School Health, 73,* 121–126.

Slowinski, J. (2000, January). Breaking the language barrier: How technology can enhance multicultural communication. *Electronic School,* National School Board Association. Retrieved January 9, 2009, at http://www.electronic-school.com/2000/01/0100f3.html

Small, M. (2006). Neighborhood institutions as resource brokers: Childcare centers, interorganizational ties, and resource access among the poor. *Social Problems, 53*(2), 274–292.

Smith, T. M., Desimone, L. M., & Ueno, K. (2006). "Highly qualified" to do what? The relationship between NCLB teacher quality mandates and the use of reform-oriented instruction in middle school mathematics. *Educational Evaluation and Policy Analysis, 27,* 75–109.

Snyder, J., & Patterson, G. (1987). Family interaction and delinquent behavior. In H. C. Quay (Ed.), *Handbook of juvenile delinquency* (pp. 216–243). New York: Wiley.

Spilsbury, J. (2005). Children's perceptions of the social support of neighborhood institutions and establishments. *Human Organization, 64*(2),1–15.

Stanton-Salazar, R. D. (2001). *Manufacturing hope and despair: The school and kin support networks of U.S.-Mexican youth.* New York: Teachers College Press.

Stewart, S. D. (2003). Nonresident parenting and adolescent adjustment: The quality of nonresident father-child interaction. *Journal of Family Issues, 24,* 217–244.

Swap, S. (1993). *Developing home-school partnerships: From concepts to practice.* New York: Teachers College Press.

Sweetland, S. R., & Hoy, W. K. (2000). School characteristics and educational outcomes: Toward an organizational model of student achievement in middle schools. *Educational Administration Quarterly, 36,* 703–729.

Tamis-LeMonda, C., & Cabrera, N. (2002). *Handbook of father involvement: Multidisciplinary perspectives.* Mahwah, NJ: Erlbaum.

Taylor, B. M., Pearson, P. D., Clark, K. F., & Walpole, S. (1999). *Beating the odds in teaching all children to read.* Center for the Improvement of Early Reading Achievement Report 2–006. Ann Arbor, MI: University of Michigan.

Taylor, D. (1983). *Family literacy: Young children learning to read and write.* Portsmouth, NH: Heinemann.

Taylor, D., & Dorsey-Gaines, C. (1988). *Growing up literate: Learning from inner-city families.* Portsmouth, NH: Heinemann.

Taylor, L., & Adelman, H. S. (2000). Connecting schools, families, and communities. *Professional School Counseling, 3,* 298–307.

Teale, W. H. (1986). Home background and young children's literacy development. In W. H. Teale & E. Sulzby (Eds.), *Emergent literacy: Writing and reading* (pp. 173–206). Norwood, NJ: Ablex.

Teddlie, C., & Reynolds, D. (2000). *The international handbook of school effectiveness research.* London: Falmer Press.

Turnbull, A. P., Turnbull, H. R., III, Shank, M., & Leal, D. (1995). *Exceptional lives: Special education in today's schools.* Englewood Cliffs, NJ: Prentice Hall, Inc.

U.S. Census Bureau. (2002). *Poverty in the United States: 2002.* Washington, DC: Author.

U.S. Department of Education. (2004). *Parental involvement: Title I, Part A. Non-Regulatory guidance.* Washington, DC: Author.

U.S. Department of Education. (2005). *Biennial evaluation report to Congress on the implementation of the state grant formula program.* Washington, DC: Author.

U.S. Department of Education. (2007). *Engaging parents in education: Lessons from five parental information and resource centers.* Retrieved September 4, 2007, from http://www.ed.gov/admins/comm/parents/parentinvolve/report

U.S. Department of Education, National Center for Education Statistics. (1997). *Fathers' involvement in their children's schools.* NCES 98-091. C. W. Nord, D. Brimhall, & J. West. Washington, DC: author.

U.S. Department of Health and Human Services. (2006). *The 2006 HHS poverty guidelines.* Retrieved August 19, 2008, at http://aspe.hhs.gov/POVERTY/06poverty.shtml

U.S. Department of Labor. (2005). *A profile of the working poor, 2003.* Washington, DC: Author.

Valadez, J. R. (2002). The influence of social capital on mathematics course selection by Latino high school students. *Hispanic Journal of Behavioral Sciences, 24,* 319–339.

Van Voorhis, F. L. (2003). Interactive homework in middle school: Effects on family involvement and science achievement. *Journal of Educational Research, 96,* 323–338.

Van Voorhis, F. L. (2007, April). *Can math be more meaningful: Longitudinal effects of family involvement on student homework.* Paper presented at the annual meeting of the American Educational Research Association (AERA) in Chicago, Illinois.

Van Voorhis, F. L., & Sheldon, S. B. (2004). Principals' roles in the development of U.S. programs of school, family, and community partnerships. *International Journal of Educational Research, 41,* 55–70.

Vedantam, S. (2005, January 23). See no bias. *Washington Post,* p. W12. Retrieved August 15, 2008, at http://www.washingtonpost.com/wp-dyn/articles/A27067-2005Jan21_4.html

Von Secker, C. (2004). Science achievement in social contexts: Analysis from National Assessment of Educational Progress. *Journal of Educational Research, 98,* 67–78.

Vulliamy, G., & Webb, R. (2003). Supporting disaffected pupils: Perspectives from the pupils, their parents and their teachers. *Educational Research, 45,* 275–286.

Warren, M. (2005). Communities and schools: A new view of urban education reform. *Harvard Educational Review, 75*(2), 133–175.

Wasik, B. A. (1998). Volunteer tutoring programs in reading: A review. *Reading Research Quarterly, 33,* 266–292.

Weinberg, C., & Weinberg, L. (1992). Multiple perspectives on the labeling, treatment, and disciplining of at-risk students. *Journal of Humanistic Education and Development, 30,* 146–156.

Weiss, C. H. (1995). Nothing as practical as good theory: Exploring theory-based evaluation for comprehensive community initiatives for children and families. In J. P. Connell, A. C. Kubisch, L. B. Schorr, & C. H. Weiss (Eds.), *New approaches to evaluating community initiatives: Concepts, methods, and contexts* (pp. 65–92). Washington, DC: The Aspen Institute, Roundtable on Comprehensive Community Initiatives for Children and Families.

Weiss, C. H. (1998). Have we learned anything new about the use of evaluation? *American Journal of Evaluation, 19,* 21–33.

Weiss, H., Kreider, H., Lopez, M., & Chatman, C. (2005). *Preparing educators to involve families.* Thousand Oaks, CA: Sage.

Westat and Policy Studies Associates. (2001). *The longitudinal evaluation of school change and performance in Title I Schools* (Vol. 1, Executive summary). Washington DC: U.S. Department of Education.

Wilson, W. J. (1987). *The truly disadvantaged: The inner-city, the underclass and public policy.* Chicago: University of Chicago Press.

Yan, W., & Lin, Q. (2005). Parent involvement and mathematics achievement: Contrast across racial and ethnic groups. *Journal of Educational Research, 99,* 116–127.

Youngs, P. (2007). How elementary principals' beliefs and actions influence new teachers' experiences. *Educational Administration Quarterly, 43,* 101–137.

Ziesemer, C. (1984). Student and staff perceptions of truancy and court referrals. *Social Work in Education, 6,* 167–178.

Index

CORWIN

A SAGE Company

The Corwin logo—a raven striding across an open book—represents the union of courage and learning. Corwin is committed to improving education for all learners by publishing books and other professional development resources for those serving the field of PreK–12 education. By providing practical, hands-on materials, Corwin continues to carry out the promise of its motto: **"Helping Educators Do Their Work Better."**